The Magic of the Akashic Records

The Magic of the Akashic Records is a work of non-fiction. Where appropriate, names and other personal details have been changed to protect people's identities.

First Publication Date: July 2015
ISBN 978-0-473-32468-1
Wilson, Chris
The Magic of the Akashic Records / Chris Wilson.
1. Spirituality—Non-Fiction 2. Metaphysics —Non-Fiction
3. Psychology—Non-Fiction

Layout, design, and typography by Lee Johnson
Cover design by Lee Johnson: 'The Book Enabler'
www.leejohnsonwriter.com

Cover photograph: While every reasonable effort has been made to establish ownership of this image, we were not able to establish the identity of the copyright holder. We consequently invite the copyright holder to contact us so that we can discuss this issue.

The Magic of the Akashic records

Understanding Our Soul Journey

Chris Wilson

Dedication

To my father David who left his body on 3/03/2013:

You taught me to use my mind to question and to learn. You brought out the best and the worst in me and helped me to find a path to joy. You have supported me throughout the writing of this book and, although you are now in spirit, are the best editor and proof reader (ghost writer) I know.

To Alice:

Without you this book would not have been possible. Your challenges led me to the Akashic Records and reunited me with my soul. Thank you for giving me permission to share your story. You are truly an inspiration.

To Marty, Hugh and Mary:

For your love, encouragement and support. You are my 'dream team' and I love you very much.

Acknowledgements

Thank you to all those who have given me permission to share their soul information and stories.

My thanks and gratitude go to:

Simon Delahunt, my editor who immersed himself in my writing and helped me to create the final product.

Bernadette Logue who advised me on book publication.

Lee Johnson who held my hand in the final stages and brought this book to fruition.

And also to the following people:

Donna Falconer and Herman de Groot: Layout and graphics.

My sister, Jenny, Sarah Wilson, Martin Wilson, Sue Wildash and Jane Grant: Proof reading and editing.

Introduction

As I have been writing this, my own **Akashic Record** (the story of my **soul**) has been open. I hope that all who read this book will be touched by the magical energy of the Records and that through its words you will come to see and understand a bigger picture of life.

Thank you to my family and friends and the many clients who have graciously allowed me to share their soul information. Extracts from their Akashic Readings have been italicised and indented in the text. In most cases names have been changed to protect identities.

At the back of this book there is a *Glossary* of words which may require further explanation. These are marked in **bold** the first time they are used.

The *Magic of the Akashic Records* is intended for those who are new to this subject as well as those who have an in-depth understanding of it. As we move from a **Third** to a **Fifth Dimensional** energy on Earth I am aware that we are experiencing all 'lifetimes' simultaneously. With my linear mindset and chronological way of thinking I find this a difficult concept to grasp and suspect that most of my readers will as well. Because of this I have used the term, '**past lives**' throughout the text.

From the readings I have given, a clear pattern has emerged. Many of those drawn to my work are **starseeds** with a soul trajectory on Earth beginning in **Lemuria**, continuing in **Atlantis** and often including Ancient Egypt, Greece, life at the time of Christ, the Dark Ages and World War II. The information in the reading extracts in the book reflects this trend.

I realise that what I have written could be controversial. The Akashic Records and my experiences in recent years have taught me the importance of living and speaking my truth. I am no longer afraid to do this. What I have said will not resonate with everyone. I respect the right of the book's readers to their own opinions and their own truth.

I am thrilled to be able share the magic of the Akashic Records with you. Have fun in the Records!

Chris Wilson
June 2015

Contents

Chapter 1

The secret's out!

I have a secret. It's too good to keep to myself! I have been working and playing in the Akashic Records for the last four years and they have transformed my life! I have cast off demons from this and other lifetimes. I have let go of fear and come home to love. My life has gone from tragic to magic!

The Akashic Records are our soul stories. They are an energetic record of every event, thought and feeling that has ever happened to each soul in existence. They are a cosmic computer which holds the details and memories of every experience ever had by every soul on Earth, a search engine where we can 'google' soul information and find out about past lives, present potentials and future possibilities.

The word *akashic* comes from the **Sanskrit** word 'akasha.' The Akashic Records exist in a higher vibrational frequency which can be accessed by those with the intention to use the information for the highest good of themselves and others.

The Akashic Records are a healing space—a place where anything is possible. They are a haven of peace and tranquility— much needed at this time of change and turmoil. They are a place where magic happens, where miracles can happen and where we can dramatically change our human lives for the better. Within the Akashic Records we can commune with our soul, see ourselves as we really are and align with our life plan.

I give readings and facilitate healing in the Akashic Records and their powerful energy has made its presence felt in my life and in the lives of those I work with.

A family crisis led me to the Records. At the age of 18 my eldest daughter developed a serious mental illness and had the first of many suicide attempts. Being a mother is my greatest joy and I am very proud of my three children, Alice, Hugh and Mary who, at the time of writing are aged 25, 23 and 19. Alice was born when I was 30 and from then on parenthood became a top priority in my life. I was devoted and conscientious; wanting only the best for my children. I wanted them to grow up with high self-esteem—the one thing I lacked as a child.

My earliest memories are of feeling there was something wrong with me and of struggling to love and accept myself. Over time I learned to cloak myself in a veneer of self-confidence but underneath I never felt lovable or good enough. I remember thinking when I met my husband, Marty, 36 years ago, that once he found out the truth about me he would leave. I carried a deep sense of shame, a belief that everything was my fault and a crippling feeling of unworthiness. Since I have been accessing my Akashic Record I have discovered the root of these feelings in my immediate past life and in others but I didn't have this understanding as a child. A deep sense of unease and feelings of intense self-hatred pervaded my childhood.

In 1989, when I held Alice in my arms, all I wanted was for her to grow up loving and believing in herself. I was determined to do everything I could to make this happen. Alice's early years were happy ones. She was joined by Hugh in 1991 and Mary in 1996. My husband was a lawyer and we had a comfortable life. I loved being a mother and adored my children. I have many happy memories from those years and of Alice's early life in particular. She was small, dark haired and pretty. The first year of her life I was on a high. I rejoiced in her accomplishments and celebrated every milestone. This beautiful, perfect child was the best thing that had ever happened to me. I felt like the luckiest woman alive. For the next few years I enjoyed the hustle and bustle of a busy household, juggling parenting with part-time work from home and soaking up the love of my children.

Yet, by the time Alice was six, it was obvious she was going down the same path I had walked as a child. She was sensitive, had low self-esteem and was bullied at school; she became shut down and withdrawn, particularly when away from home. One of the hardest things as a parent is seeing your child suffer. It is even harder when you can feel their pain because you have been there yourself.

When Alice was ten, I was ready to return to full-time work. I wanted a flexible job that I felt passionate about. I developed a conscious parenting programme, *The Heart to Heart Course for Parents* which I have since taught to hundreds of people. It helped me greatly. I faced my fears, was able to lay some childhood issues to rest and gained confidence in public speaking and facilitating groups. Putting myself out there week after week helped me to feel a greater sense of self-worth. I read parenting books avidly and did my best to 'walk my talk.' The course was about love rather than fear based parenting and was designed to build up the self-esteem of parents and children.

At school Alice excelled academically. She had close relationships with her teachers and was involved in a wide range of activities but still did not love or even like herself. While Alice was a teenager I kept on working, trying to ignore the early rumblings of the storm which hit our family with full force in 2007. One week she was radiant in a bright pink dress, dancing at her school leavers' ball, the next, after two suicide attempts, she was locked in a secure facility for adolescent psychiatric patients. I was heartbroken. I hadn't seen this coming and could not understand how or why it had happened.

In the Akashic Records I have found the answers I was seeking and much, much more. I first used the Akashic Records to find my own information, then to answer questions for friends. The information resonated and was helpful. Word spread, I started giving readings to others and now it is my full-time job.

There have been so many positive spin offs for myself and others from my work in the Records that I feel I have to tell the world ! The energy in the Akashic Records is uplifting and vibrant. The words that come to me are loving, non-judgmental and high in vibration. Just being in the Records is healing. Clients tell me that they feel the energising power of the Records during a session and that it lingers afterwards and sets in motion a positive chain of events—their lives improve as if by magic. I spend so much time in the Records that I can vouch for their healing properties. One of the best parts of my job is that every time I go into the Records to help someone else I am helping myself as well.

It is hard to remember myself as the person who cried most nights from 2007 to 2010, whose health packed up with stress and who lurched from one drama to the next, compulsively talking about her problems. I have changed from the mother who saw her child as something that needed fixing and pulled out all the stops to save her. This experience has forced me to face my deepest fears, insecurities and shame, helped me overcome a recurring soul pattern of victimhood and move into a place of strength, courage and self-love. I am grateful to Alice for this gift and also know that the Akashic Records have helped me to ride the waves and safely reach the shore.

The Akashic Records are a soul space. The more time I spend there the more aligned I am becoming with my true self. I am able to see the bigger picture of this lifetime and its challenges and understand and know who I really am. I am working in my own Akashic Record to let go of all that has limited me in this and other lifetimes and am helping others to do the same. A friend says when she is in her Record, she feels like she's "wrapped in a warm blanket." The energy is gentle and nurturing, compassionate and soothing. The Akashic Records are a portal to a special place and a safe container for healing to occur.

For a long time our collective consciousness has held the belief that we have to do things the hard way. Beliefs like, 'I am not good enough, life is a struggle, I deserve to suffer,' have prevailed and created a reality where life has been challenging and complicated. Locked into our human belief system has been a fundamental tenet that we can only grow through suffering. I always suspected that life could be easier. The good news is that I am right—we no longer need to endure pain and suffering to evolve. We can do it with ease and grace by getting into the flow of the Akashic Records and accessing their timeless wisdom.

If I was to choose the greatest gift the Records have given me, it is inner peace. They have helped me detach from drama and attachment to anything that has happened in the past or that may happen in the future. I am now (mostly) firmly rooted in the present and able to stay peaceful, calm and joyful no matter what is happening around me. For someone who has been fearful for most of her life and still has a daughter who struggles daily, this is no mean feat. Now for the first time in my life (many lives in fact!) I feel like my soul self and my personality self are working in partnership, in tandem. The potential for what we can create together is huge. There is more excitement, joy and anticipation in my life than I ever thought possible. I am a better person, more authentic and compassionate and less judgmental. Everything about my life has improved.

As well as having a greater feeling of well-being and peace, the Akashic Records have helped to raise my energy and heighten my intuition. I give readings to people from all over the world. The hardest person to read for is myself. I know myself so well that it is easy for my mind to get in the way. Often I question the information I get and think, "I already knew that." However if I put it to one side for a few days and then read it again I always find it is profound and exactly what I needed to hear. For email readings all I have to go on is a name and some questions. I always feel a knot of panic when I read words from someone who I don't know and will never meet, especially when they ask big questions like, "What is my **life purpose**?" or about the future of a relationship they are in. It is a huge responsibility and one I take very seriously. These readings have helped me to trust the information I receive and this, set against a backdrop of the ancient energy of the Records has heightened my intuition and helped me in all areas of my life. I now have a much stronger sense of direction and an inner voice I can trust. I can tune in and get clear and helpful answers. This has made my life much easier.

When I am writing I open my own Record before I begin and it helps with the process. This and future books already exist in my Akashic Record so I make it easy for myself. An artist friend says his work has improved since he has been painting within his Akashic Record. The energy of the Records amplifies any activity taking place within it—it enhances any creative process. I run Soul History workshops teaching others to find answers within their Akashic Records and to facilitate their own healing. Many of the **lightworkers** who have attended these go into their Records before client sessions and say it has taken their work to a new level. As if this isn't enough, the Records can be used to let go of all that is holding us back. I have been using mine to free myself from lifetimes of limitation and have found that within that sacred space, with trust and intention, anything is possible.

I am a starseed. One of a group of souls from other parts of the **Milky Way Galaxy** who approximately 100,000 years ago, agreed to come to Earth to anchor **codes of light** and to help activate a

twelve-strand DNA human potential. In her book, *The Sunshine before the Dawn*, Judy Satori tells the story of these souls who chose to help at this time of changing consciousness on Earth. We undertook to live many Earth lifetimes and to experience all aspects of being human. Part of our contract was to be here to play an active role at this crucial time when we are moving from a Third to a Fifth Dimensional planet.

History has always fascinated me. When I was studying for my Masters and then teaching History to teenage girls in the 1980s, I never dreamed that one day Soul History would be my subject. My thesis was a dry account of an aspect of 18th century English political history, written to please a lecturer I loved. I didn't realise all those years ago that my passion for history might be because I have been a part of it. For thousands of years my soul's history has been intertwined with that of Earth. Along the way I have experienced light and dark, good and evil, happiness and sadness.

As has been the lot of starseeds who carry a vibration that many have found threatening, I have attracted persecution and suffering. The 'Dark Ages' were very dark for me. On this journey I have created **karma** and picked up some distorted and negative beliefs and behaviour patterns. I understand that an important part of my life purpose this time has been to release and transcend my fears and these tendencies. Alice's illness has been a catalyst for this and the Akashic Records are providing a safe space for me to let go of all that no longer serves me. I have always intuitively known there is a better way and this is it!

Working in the Akashic Records to let go of limitation is simple and painless. A certain degree of self-awareness is necessary as a foundation for this work but those I am teaching these techniques to, in workshops and on Skype, are not afraid of working on themselves. They now have the tools to free themselves of any limiting beliefs, sabotaging patterns, fears and negative feelings they are ready to discard. Not only do these techniques work quickly, they are empowering. We can use them to help ourselves as the need arises without seeking outside help. This is the beauty of the Akashic Records. They relieve our suffering and we are in charge of the process! This may sound too good to be true. Those who have felt the benefits—myself included—know that it isn't.

In workshops I prepare participants to open their Akashic Record by taking them on a guided visualisation to the **Hall of Records**. This is usually an enjoyable experience as I talk the group through meeting loved ones at the entrance and being escorted inside by their guide. At one workshop, at the end of this exercise, a young woman called Helen asked if it was normal to feel anxious. As she said this I noticed she was shivering uncontrollably, had sweat pouring off her face and was in the throes of a full-blown panic attack. I quickly opened Helen's Akashic Record and demonstrated the healing technique I had planned to teach later in the day, guiding her through a process to release her anxiety. Before our eyes she was transformed as the trembling stopped, her heart rate slowed and she became calm and peaceful.

It was a dramatic transformation and an excellent example for us all of what is possible in the Records. When I followed up with Helen afterwards she told me that a question she had asked, "Why do I always give my power away?" triggered the attack. She is a soul who has experienced much past life trauma and had been feeling fearful and unable to move forward in her life. This situation gave her the opportunity to let go of anxiety and some of the feelings that had been keeping her stuck.

I have been working with a client, Kerry, who came to me suffering from severe depression and deep anxiety. Since the age of 30 she has played out a repeated pattern where things go well for a while and then fall apart. I found she has a soul history of self-destruction and that this lifetime is about breaking this pattern.

When she came to me she had just lost her job and was at an all time low. I worked with her to find the past life origins of this entrenched behaviour and to clear her anxiety, negative beliefs and thoughts. She was eager to learn how to access her Akashic Record so she could continue this work herself. She has been working consistently in the Records and it is paying off. When she had her initial session her partner was overseas on a three week trip. On his return he was astounded and delighted at the change in her. She also noticed a change immediately. In her words:

"I felt much more positive. My dark thoughts were gone. My anxiety was gone. I am now sleeping well, am more relaxed and detached from drama and can express myself better … If I meditate in the Akashic Records I can get into a place of deep relaxation very quickly. I feel a kind of forgiveness—a wanting to be more gentle with myself—and feel far more motivated in my everyday life … I am more confident and less paranoid around certain people—I know I can go into my Record and ask about 'other lives' we have spent together—and can uncover the deeper reasons for my trepidation. I am enjoying life again. Being with people is easier. There is more lightness and laughter, and a greater sense of purpose."

Kerry recently returned to the workforce. She had a choice of two jobs. One was with a company she has been temping for, working under a notoriously difficult manager. She chose the other job but said she had amazed herself (and others as well) with the way she had handled her 'difficult' boss. She has been dipping into the Akashic Records for a while now so can stay in them for long periods. Kerry told me she does this at the start of every day and that it is helping her cope with her new job and in all areas of her life. Recently she told me she was lying awake one night unable to sleep, not as has often happened before, because she was anxious, but rather because feelings of excitement and anticipation were keeping her awake. Thinking back over her day she remembered she had forgotten to close her Akashic Record. She did this and was soon fast asleep.

The healing potential of the Records is very exciting! As soon as we open our Akashic Record we are transported to a high and loving vibration. I am learning through my work that the Akashic Records are not only an etheric source of information accessed through words but are also held in the cells of our bodies and in the energy field surrounding our bodies. As the Earth raises its frequency, the incoming light is activating layers within our so-called 'junk' DNA. It is also activating the imprints held within our energy fields from other soul experiences and awakening our Akashic Record which is stored at a cellular and molecular level. This is opening up a potential to work within our Akashic Record with the intelligence of every cell of our body to heal the emotional and physical **dis-ease** we carry from our current and previous lifetimes. This soul/cell healing is, I believe, the way of the future. I discuss this in more detail in Chapters 10-12.

Using the Akashic Records to gain information and to heal is powerful and unquestionably facilitates personal transformation. The true magic of the Akashic Records, however, is what Kryon (a being channelled by Lee Carroll) calls 'Mining the Akash.' Within our Akashic Record we can reconnect with our gifts, talents and wisdom from other lifetimes. Once we have mastered a lesson or skill the knowledge stays with us for eternity. I am teaching others how to re-discover and reap the benefits of the gold along their soul timeline and am doing this for myself. It is truly life-changing.

There are so many ways the Akashic Records can help us. They are a godsend. The benefits I have described are, I believe, just the tip of the iceberg. I encourage those I teach to adapt the Records to help them in their lives. Feedback, such as this extract from an email from a client is heartening:

"I am still going extremely well. The changes within myself and

my family are nothing short of miraculous. These techniques really do work!"

Reincarnation, or the belief that we live many lives in different bodies, has always resonated with me. In order to evolve, our soul chooses a variety of life experiences. The goal is **Mastery** where we have learned the human lessons, 'passed our exams' and can choose whether we return to Earth or continue our evolution elsewhere.

Our soul selves are clamouring to be heard. As the veil between Heaven and Earth is thinning, we are coming home to our true natures. The heightened energies as we make the transition from a Third Dimensional to a Fifth Dimensional planet are accelerating this. These are exciting times! Like a wise and knowing parent, our soul wants the best for us and against our will encourages us to do what is necessary to evolve. Our soul knows our life plan and contracts and how they fit in with all that has gone before. It knows what karma we wish to address, the unfinished business we would like to complete, our chosen life lessons and purpose. It holds the vision for what we hope to achieve and what we need to do to bring ourselves into balance. A key part of our soul's agenda is about healing the past. It sees the bigger picture and will always point us in the direction of healing.

Our human self has a different motive. It has a short term view which usually involves playing it safe and avoiding suffering at all costs. Our soul's aim is mastery. It leads us, like a stubborn teenager, kicking and screaming into life situations that are for our highest good. Our soul knows the experiences we have chosen and what is necessary for growth. It is tough love that throws up many challenges but like any devoted parent, it keeps cheering us on. Loving us unconditionally, our soul wants only the best for us.

My experiences with Alice have taught me that when, in human terms, things fall apart, on a soul level it is perfect. What makes little sense on a human level makes total sense in the light of the

Records. This has been my main learning in the Akashic Records and is a priceless gift. Their beauty is that they can transport us from our human misery and inertia to a higher vantage point where we can see the bigger picture and understand the reasons behind our life choices and challenges. This soul information buoys us up and gives us the courage to carry on.

It is a privilege to do this work. I see my clients as the souls they are—beings of courage and limitless potential, and reflect this back to them. I connect with the highest vision for their current lifetime, their highest potential and possibilities and pass this on. I am working and relating soul to soul. An Akashic reading is an uplifting experience for most because I am working in a compassionate, loving energy and the information given is positive and constructive. The fear and torment that characterise life in a human body can be put to one side and we can view our lives from a more expansive viewpoint. We are teleported out of our human-ness and reconnected to the loving and soothing presence that is our soul. This is of immense value to those I work with who mostly want to know whether they are on track with their life's plan and what they can do to live their life purpose and reach their potential.

The Akashic Records are teaching me about the relationship between our human and soul selves. We have lived many lifetimes of **duality** where human conflict and the ensuing suffering have reigned supreme. Along the way there has been a split between our spiritual and our human aspects. Rather than working together in harmony they have been at odds with one another. The Akashic Records can help us bring these two parts back into alignment. When this happens the potentials for the future and what it is possible to co-create are huge.

In a reading with a client, Suzanne, I found she was waking up to her spiritual nature after many lifetimes. She asked why she was being drawn to spirituality and, as is the case for many of us, I found that her life was planned in two parts. In the first her human side would dominate and in the second her soul would make its presence felt.

> *This is a time of exploration for you and a time of reconnecting to your soul core and your soul's plan for this lifetime so you can take a different direction.*

> *You have planned your life in two distinct parts ... the first is a conventional path where you have been having a human experience, retracing steps from many past lives and giving you the opportunity to release and process many of these. The second marks the return of your soul and authentic self. This part of you is propelling you in a more spiritual direction. There is a deep yearning for your soul to be recognised and reintegrated into your life and this is what is happening now.*

As is often the case, Suzanne's life experience has prepared her for the work she plans to do in the future:

> *You are on the brink of an exciting and interesting time. You have work to do which will be completely different from your current work... it is your soul work and involves storytelling in a way that will help others to understand their spiritual path and journey and bring their human and soul selves into balance. Your work will enable others to embrace their spiritual aspects and to bring them into harmony with their human selves. This has been and will be your journey and will be what you share with others. In doing this you will reconnect with a part of yourself you rejected in a past life where for self-protection, you shut down your spiritual nature. This will enable you to reclaim your spiritual side and to do some deep soul healing.*

> *The first part of your life has been about experiencing and releasing on the level of the personality and the second part is*

about embracing yourself as a spiritual being, at the level of the soul.

I have read many books about near death experiences and our re-entry into the spirit world and have come to the conclusion that being in the Akashic Records is as near as possible to Heaven on Earth. We are able to sample the flavour of Heaven while on Earth and it tastes divine!

The Akashic Records are a bridge between the physical and spiritual realms which allow us to rediscover and merge with our soul. They can help us off-load the baggage we have picked up in many lifetimes and bring us home to our true selves. In the Records we commune and reconnect with our souls. Like lovers reunited after a breakup, fuelled by passion and joy, this combined energy of soul and personality can empower us and take us to new heights. When we work in the Akashic Records, in conscious partnership with our soul anything is possible.

———————————————————————————————

Chapter 2
Prelude

I have always known that I have lived before, in other times, in other places and in other bodies. When I was very young, I remember thinking to myself, "I must get it right this time. I have got to get it right this time." I came into this world with a knowing that this lifetime was special, that I had a job to do and that it was vitally important that I do it. As a child I spent many hours wondering about the mystery of life and asking myself questions like, "Where do I come from? Why am I here? What is my purpose? What part do I have to play?"

I knew I wasn't alone, yet I often felt very alone. I knew I was a part of something much bigger, something magnificent that was out there but was somehow just beyond my reach. I knew this lifetime was of crucial importance and that I had to stick to my contract. On a deeper level I understood that I had been here many times before and that I had often deviated from my life plan in ways that had harmed myself and others.

From the day I was born I carried an energy of guilt and shame which was easy for people to exploit. In my adult life, in using my gift for accessing the Akashic Records, I have come to understand the reasons for the shame and self-loathing I had as a child and for my feelings of powerlessness. I was born saying "sorry." The fourth and twin daughter in a family of five girls, I was a surprise. My mother had already had one set of twins six years earlier when my eldest sister was born with her stillborn twin brother. The elderly doctor in our New Zealand town had not realised my mother was carrying twins until she went into early labour. Not long before the birth she had a fall and she thinks this is how she lost her son. Another daughter, Margaret, had been born three years later and now, in 1958, my mother was pregnant again with what she thought was one child, hopefully a boy.

Again, her doctor had not picked twins although my mother has said she had her suspicions. Once more she went into labour prematurely and produced not one but two babies. My sister, Jennifer, was born first and ten minutes later I arrived. My mother has always said she felt clever and proud to have produced healthy twins. When my father was alive he talked of the shock of his family doubling overnight and of having to take out a mortgage for additions to the house he had built when he got married. I was not expected but loved and welcomed nevertheless.

Despite this, my introduction to this lifetime was traumatic and difficult. A premature baby, I was taken from the security and comfort of my mother and sister to a cold incubator where I spent six weeks. With the knowledge I have now and my ability to access my Akashic Record, I realise that this experience activated beliefs that I carried from my most recent life and in particular the thoughts I had as I lay dying. I have discovered that my last life ended in the early 1950s in Germany and that I died an unhappy and tormented man. Like millions I was a victim of Hitler's Third Reich, but a German victim. An earnest young man from a southern part of Germany, well away from Berlin, I was a Catholic priest when the war began and managed to distance myself from it at first. Towards the end of the war, bureaucracy caught up with me and I was drafted and dispatched to a concentration camp as an SS officer. I had three choices, to fight at the front as a soldier, to help run a camp or be imprisoned in a camp. I chose the second option as I felt it gave me the greatest chance of survival.

I saved my life but destroyed my soul. I did not know what I was letting myself in for. It was a living hell and although I did my best to work on assigned tasks where I didn't have to harm people, as a soldier of the Third Reich I was expected to follow orders and I did. I tried to help some inmates even though it would mean certain death but I was never brave enough to challenge the regime whose brutality sickened me. I volunteered to work in the crematorium and spent days supervising the burning of bodies. I did my best to treat the dead with dignity and prayed as I worked but I was in a concentration camp: I knew what was happening and I did nothing to stop it. Fear of my own death stopped me and it is ironic that I did not survive for long after the war— I lost my will to live. I could not forgive myself for what I had done and for what I had been a part of, became depressed and took to my bed. My family loved me but could not get through to me. No one could reach me. I was deeply depressed and riddled with shame, guilt and self-hatred.

There was only a short gap between that past life and this one and the emotions I felt as I died, alone and heartbroken, were easily and quickly, reactivated in this lifetime when I found myself back in a human body, alone in an incubator. I came into this world carrying a heavy load and a deep feeling of unworthiness. In childhood photographs I am serious and unsmiling. I remember feeling that there was something wrong with me and that everything was somehow my fault.

Not surprisingly this attracted negative experiences. I was lucky to have my four sisters and loving parents who created a secure and stable home environment. My youngest sister, Susan, was born when Jennifer and I were four. As a child I was often the scapegoat. It was as if I had the word 'victim' inscribed on my forehead and I see now that I set myself up for this. I was sensitive and an easy target.

It was comforting having Jenny in my life. She was a constant companion and we were different but close. She has always been a very loving and loyal friend as well as sibling. She approached life differently to me with a confidence and brashness that I didn't have. Although we were labelled 'the twins' we were always compared. I was the quiet one, Jenny the noisy one; I was the shy one, Jenny the outgoing one; I was the good one, Jenny the naughty one.

I admired Jenny's gregarious nature, her lack of respect for those who didn't earn it, her courage and honesty and the way she challenged people. At age five we started school and on the second day she went to the bathroom. While she was there she noticed long loops of toilet paper on the floor. A teacher came in just as she was leaving, saw the paper and accused Jenny of unrolling it. Jenny has a strong sense of justice and has never been able to tolerate being wrongly accused. She was very upset and stormed back into the classroom leaving the door open. Our teacher—a strict spinster who seemed ancient to us—told Jenny to shut the door. My sister, still smarting from the toilet paper incident said, "Shut it yourself!"

I watched in horror as our teacher, skirts flying, chased Jenny around the room with a long stick, eventually catching up with her and repeatedly beating her on the legs. Jenny defiantly held out her chin showing no fear or sadness. Not one tear rolled down her face but I was a blubbering mess. That incident had a profound effect on me. I was terrified and very upset. I realise now why I was so affected. I was a small child and this incident most likely triggered subconscious memories of my most recent past life where to be singled out, to defy authority and to speak out meant certain death. Past life trauma was activated on that day for both of us. Jenny's most recent past life was as a British POW building the Burma Railway during World War II. She was a leader and fought against unjust treatment in the camps, dying of malnutrition and starvation shortly before liberation.

Jenny and I have shared many lifetimes. I was so traumatised by my experiences as a German soldier that I didn't want to enter this life alone and chose to be supported by an old soul-mate in a twin/sibling relationship. Two souls connected through time with very different, recent soul histories. One a coward, the other a hero.

By the age of six, Jenny and I were at a new school and were moved into a class where I met Phoebe. I was captivated. To me she was beautiful. She had thick blonde hair and was good at everything. I put her on a pedestal and did anything she wanted for the next 11 years. I gave my power away to her completely and let myself be manipulated, controlled and abused by her. It seemed natural to follow her orders. Some days, particularly when we were on our own, we would have a wonderful time and I would feel special and appreciated. This never lasted and when others were around I was always the butt of jokes and the one on the outer. I followed her, desperate for approval and for any crumb of love and acceptance. This blighted my childhood and eroded my fragile self-esteem even further.

My family couldn't understand the hold Phoebe had over me and neither could I but it was strong and it was real and I followed her around allowing myself to be treated badly. I was like a faithful dog, waiting and expecting to be kicked and coming back for more. My teenage years were agonising as I found it impossible to break away from this 'friendship.' As a teenager, Phoebe was the coolest girl in our year group with a large following. I chose to remain a part of this elitist group albeit on the fringes. It was a living hell. I let myself be the victim of bullying and the scapegoat for the frustrations of Phoebe and her group.

It was a difficult situation. The classes at our school were strictly streamed according to ability. Jenny and I were always in the top stream (or class) and so was Phoebe. There was no escape and she reigned supreme. Jenny chose to opt out of this group and was ostracised for it. She had a miserable time at secondary school. We were both unhappy. I have always admired Jenny for the stand she took. She may have been lonely but at least she had her self-respect.

Being part of Phoebe's group was soul destroying. Just as I had in Germany, I acted in a way that didn't match my true values and beliefs. I gave my power away and I hated myself for it. It was only years later during a past life regression that I fully understood this relationship. Phoebe had been my superior officer at the concentration camp I was assigned to. No wonder I had done whatever she wanted and followed her blindly and without reason.

I always loved reading. I found it a great way to escape reality and often visited our town library. As a teenager I stopped reading fiction and became fixated on just two types of material—books about spirituality, particularly those with evidence of life after death, and books on the Holocaust. By the 1970s, thirty years had elapsed since World War II and many survivors were telling their stories. I read and suffered through every one. I rejoiced in the stories which told of outsmarting the Nazis, of survival tactics and eventual freedom. The section describing the moment of liberation was always my favourite part of the book. The chapters detailing suffering and the many atrocities committed were harrowing for me but I felt compelled to read on.

In many ways my childhood was not a happy or an easy one and my experiences reinforced and strengthened my feelings of shame and self-hatred. Maybe there was a karmic aspect to this as I chose to experience powerlessness just as my holocaust victims had done. Despite this, there was always a part of me that was removed and looking on, a part of me that believed in myself and in the crucial importance of this lifetime to make a contribution to humanity. I have always had an inner knowing and connection to my soul potential and have carried the memory of many lifetimes with me. During the darkest days of my childhood I knew intuitively that there was a higher reason for my experiences and that I would come through this and be able to help others.

When I was seventeen a wonderful thing happened. I had heard for years about the AFS exchange programme and I decided to apply. There have been a few things in my life that I have just known I had to do and this was one of them. I was a hard worker who despite my shyness played an active part in school life. I filled out my application and did my best to push all feelings of inadequacy aside during the interview. It was as if something took over. I knew it had gone well and was not surprised when I was one of the few awarded a scholarship. This was a watershed year for me. I lived with a lovely family in a dormitory suburb of San Francisco. Away from Phoebe and all that was familiar I started to find my own identity and to reconnect with my power. The seeds of self-belief started to germinate—I began to enjoy life and to dream.

I returned to New Zealand happier and more confident and started university. The next few years were wonderful as I worked to gain a Master of Arts in History, met my future husband, Marty, and made some close and enduring friendships. Life was easier with Marty by my side. I left university and trained as a teacher and got my first job at a girls' high school. I entered teaching as a last resort as one of the few options for history graduates. The part of me that was shy and lacking in self-worth was scared of having to stand up and speak in front of a class but after a month as a teacher I realised I was enjoying it. I really liked my pupils and their love and devotion boosted my confidence and helped me to heal and forget my past. Through accessing my Akashic Record I have since discovered that teaching is a talent I have had in many lifetimes.

This was a light-filled time in my life. I became engaged to and married Marty (who was by this time a young lawyer rapidly rising up the ranks). We started a family in 1989 and by 1996 were the parents of Alice, Hugh and Mary. I loved being a parent and was determined to do the best job I could. Wanting my children to grow up with the self-belief I had lacked, I read up on positive parenting and thought carefully about what parents could do to help their children reach their potential.

Alice was a beautiful child and an absolute delight to me. She was born looking terrified, as if she didn't want to be here but quickly adjusted and was our pride and joy. As a small child she was boisterous and unpredictable with a mind of her own. I tried to keep this in check. I was determined to be the perfect mother with the perfect child and worried about what other adults thought. Nevertheless, I did my best to parent her in a way that kept her self-esteem intact. It was a challenge because I was inexperienced and as a small child, Alice pushed the boundaries.

Despite my best efforts, from her early years at Primary School Alice struggled with shyness and was a target for bullies. Hugh and Mary had no problems with self-esteem. They were happy and believed in themselves. With my children growing up I was keen to return to work. I had loved teaching but remembering the long hours and my level of commitment to the job, I knew it would be difficult with three young children to do it justice. I looked around for suitable work and there was nothing that fitted. My passion was fostering self-esteem in children and giving them a good start in life so they could reach their potential. I had attended parenting courses including a *Positive Parenting* one which I hadn't found very positive at all. The other participants had dominated discussion, talking about everything that was wrong with their children. They never looked at themselves or the bigger picture. I could see a need for a different kind of parenting course, one that focused on the positive, on meeting children's emotional needs and helping parents prepare their children for their mission in life. One day I had a 'light bulb moment'—I would create my own parenting course and be able to help Alice, myself and others at the same time.

In 1999, *The Heart to Heart Course* designed to build up the self-esteem of parents and children was born. Many parents came to my courses and the feedback was heartening. I had a fear of speaking out to groups of adults which I knew intuitively I would have to overcome if I was to follow my life plan. I joined the local Toastmasters Club and with each course it became a little easier to stand up and speak. As I drove to my first meeting I knew I wasn't alone in the car. I could feel the supportive energy of my guides and spirit helpers and could almost hear them cheering. At the beginning of my first course as I introduced myself I felt a whoosh and surge of energy rush through me. These signs from Spirit gave me a boost and let me know I was on track.

For many years speaking to groups was nerve-racking—every Tuesday when my course sessions took place, I would be in turmoil. It was never easy. Running these courses was the best thing I could have done to build up my self-esteem and confidence. They were healing for me. As I taught the course and listened to the parents who attended, I reflected on my own childhood and was able to make sense of it. My family also benefitted as I did my best to live what I was teaching. I was a conscious parent doing work I believed in with flexible hours. In this way I was able to be a dedicated parent with my husband and children remaining central to my life.

Underpinning my new career and passion was a growing spirituality. In 1996, Mary was born. She was wise and knowing. She brought a calm and high vibrational energy into our household. Her presence in my life ushered in a new phase of spiritual exploration and discovery. I had always had a mistrust of organised religion. Sitting in a church did not do it for me. I did not like being told what to think. I had been baptised a Presbyterian and had all my babies christened as Anglicans. I knew a spiritual connection was important and had a growing yearning for one, but thought it could only happen through joining an existing church, none of which held any appeal for me. In my heart, many of the church teachings did not resonate. One day it occurred to me that it was possible to be spiritual without being religious. After that I didn't look back. I started to read self-help and psycho-spiritual books.

My husband, by this time deeply unhappy in his legal career, introduced me to authors such as Wayne Dyer and Stuart Wilde. I was on my way! Around this time my eldest sister, Judy, started spontaneously **channelling** and we shared our journeys and experiences with each other. I attended and assisted at Judy's first channelling workshops and met others with whom I could share my beliefs. I learned to meditate and incorporated spiritual practices into my daily life.

One of the key messages in my *Heart to Heart* course was that children are their parents' teachers. Alice has been, and still is, my greatest teacher. At this time my growing children were beginning to teach me about the power of cellular memory and the impact of past life trauma. At the age of five Hugh woke up screaming night after night. His eyes were glazed and he would look right through me. It was impossible to connect or communicate with him in a normal way. I would hold him until he eventually calmed down and went to sleep.

One night I was prompted to say, "You are remembering a lifetime when you were another little boy. You are Hugh, now. You are safe and no longer need to be frightened. Those men can't hurt you anymore." After I said these words he went straight back to sleep and his nightmares stopped. We were never bothered by 'night terrors' again. I consulted my sister, Judy, who said that at the same age in his most recent past life Hugh had been executed by the Khymer Rouge in Cambodia.

Mary has always been squeamish and gets very distressed at the sight of blood, particularly her own. When she was three she nearly lost her finger when a heavy door swung back and sliced it. Memories of her screams still haunt me. As a child and young teenager, she would faint in biology lessons and whenever she witnessed or heard about physical suffering. She fainted when, as part of a lesson, her diabetic teacher injected herself in front of the class. She fainted when she was listening to a talk on gangrene at our local museum. Many times I received phone calls and had to pick her up and bring her home after she had passed out. Again I talked to my sister who saw Mary in her immediate past life as a lady during the French Revolution who had witnessed the murder at the guillotine of close friends and family.

My children have taught me much and in their own ways have all helped me find my path but it has been, Alice, and her experiences as a young adult that have catapulted me to where I am now—a place from which there is no return!

As my first child and having many of the issues that marked my early life (feelings of low self-worth, anxiety, and the vibration of the victim), Alice has always been dear to my heart. I have been more involved in her life than in the lives of my other children. In recent years this has been used against me but I so wanted her childhood to be different to mine. I wanted her to grow up loving and believing in herself. I could see myself in her and feel her pain and anguish. Every step she took in life was a milestone, a new experience. I was always there by her side cheering her on, helping her, picking her up, trying to be the perfect mother, doing what all the books told me was right.

It wasn't helped by the fact that she found life difficult. The look on her face as she was born and contemplated this lifetime has come back to haunt Marty and I many times in the last few years. She was terrified from Day One. Life was always going to be a challenge. It was as if she didn't want to be here and felt she didn't belong. As a highly sensitive child, she picked up on and carried our emotional baggage. We have worked hard to lighten this over the years but poor Alice got the worst of it.

Despite all this she was a sweet and well behaved child, happiest when she was playing by herself with dolls or toys or being creative with paint or clay. She is artistically talented and her work won an award at an international children's art exhibition. She was devoted to her parents, especially me, and we loved her deeply. Looking back there were a few warning signs for what later occurred but nothing that prepared us for the way Alice's life suddenly unravelled at the age of eighteen.

At this age our beautiful daughter first tried to take her own life and the first of many incidents of serious self-harm began. We were horrified and heartbroken. Alice had never found life easy. The private girls' school we sent her to because we felt she needed support only reinforced her feelings of unworthiness and fuelled her fears. She never felt enough at that school; not good enough, or rich enough or clever enough or cool enough. We suggested moving her but she begged to stay. She loved the structure, the traditions and many of the staff who were good to her. Alice was a perfectionist and retreated into her school work in her teenage years pushing herself to excel. She became involved in many of the activities the school offered and kept herself busy. She wasn't bullied as she had been at primary school but she found friendships difficult, always staying on the fringes of groups. I tried to help her, taking her to the doctor and arranging counselling but part of me was in shock and denial and found it difficult to accept what was happening. She enrolled at Canterbury University to begin a degree in Psychology and I hoped fervently that once she left school her life would improve and she would find happiness and purpose. This wasn't to be. She took the first of many overdoses two months before the end of her final school year.

During that year her anxiety increased, she was put on medication and received regular counselling. As part of Alice's treatment we started having family therapy. This consisted of the five of us sitting in a room with a trainee therapist while her supervisor looked at us through a one-way mirror. We felt like animals in a zoo! Every week we were asked the question, 'Where are you on the hope scale?" Mary, Hugh, Marty and I would say '10/10.' Alice would say '1/10' or on a good day a '3/10.' She would often run out of the room, during a session, leaving the rest of us feeling frustrated. One day the therapist who was observing us came into the room and said we needed to do some work on how we dealt with anger. This made us angry! That night I had a visit from Mary and Hugh. They begged me to stop family therapy. They hated it. They were worried about Alice but didn't think the sessions were helping any of us. We never went back. I was very relieved!

To her credit Alice made it through to the end of the year and sat and passed her exams. As I watched Alice and Marty dance the father and daughter waltz at her school ball, I was sure the worst was behind us. I was wrong.

By the following Saturday she'd had two suicide attempts and was a patient in the adolescent psychiatric ward. Nothing had prepared me for this. I had no personal experience of mental illness and was devastated. Alice's suicide and self-harming attempts escalated and she became a stranger to us. She was haunted and severely depressed. She could not remember anything positive ever happening in her life or see anything positive in herself or anyone else, including us. She kept harming herself at every opportunity and soon her arms were covered with scars. She kept trying to kill herself. For her safety she spent much of the next two and a half years in psychiatric wards. Alice as we had known her was lost to us. We were treated with suspicion and mistrust by medical staff who placed our family and especially me under a microscope. I put myself under a magnifying glass as well. Being my first child I could remember so much—her favourite books, her achievements and her first words were indelibly etched in my mind. I lay awake night after night going over her life in my head, asking myself if it was all my fault, thinking about what I could have done differently and agonising over every little detail. I eventually came to the conclusion that nothing I had done had caused this.

I kept running my parenting courses but even though I knew I was not responsible for Alice's illness, it wasn't easy standing up talking about parenting when my own child had just had another suicide attempt. I had always been open and honest about my life experiences and with these new developments didn't feel able to be. I didn't like this lack of transparency. Here I was, someone who had lived and breathed the importance of self-esteem, who had taught many parents techniques for building up their children's self-worth, whose own child hated herself so much she wanted to die.

Chapter 3
The Search for Answers

How does a mother cope with such heartbreak? It was not easy. My health suffered. My immune system shut down. I developed asthma and allergies. I felt constantly drained and exhausted. I shed many tears and tried to understand and rationalise what had happened by talking about it to anyone who would listen. It was as if I felt I had to talk about it to believe it was really happening. It was a living nightmare. This was not the life I had wanted for Alice or for me. We lurched from one drama to another over the next few years. I was mindful of my other children and tried my best to support them and to keep family life stable and secure.

Hugh was a teenager with many friends, a drummer in a band with a part-time job. He coped by keeping himself busy away from home. Alice was his first playmate, they had been close as children and her illness affected him deeply. Alice was also very close to her younger sister, who was eleven when Alice became seriously ill. She'd always adored her and had been a devoted big sister, taking on an almost motherly role with her from the day I brought Mary home from hospital.

I tried to protect Mary from the full impact of what had happened but it wasn't easy. We were so shell-shocked we talked about it around her more than we should have. She saw me sitting in front of, and staring into, the fire crying more than she should have. She was there when the phone calls came through. Alice had escaped from the psychiatric ward, Alice had been picked up and was in the police cells, Alice had taken another overdose, Alice had cut herself badly, Alice had been attacked by a patient and her nose was broken, Alice had taken hundreds of Panadol tablets and was in intensive care, her liver was failing and she wasn't expected to live. Mary was there to hear my screams when I found Alice hanging in her bedroom and with the help of ambulance staff cut her down and saved her life.

The Alice we knew had vanished. She wasn't the sister Mary remembered. Mary had to grow up fast and she rose to the occasion. She is a special person with a loving, healing energy which helped each of us. Before this crisis, Marty and I had been pulling in different directions and beginning to drift apart. Sometimes we seemed more like siblings as we competed and bickered over trivial things. For our relationship, Alice's illness was a blessing. We grew up overnight and left most of our two year old behaviour behind. We realised what was important in life, that we loved each other and started working as a team. Many expected our marriage to fall apart as well but luckily for us Alice's illness has made it stronger.

My spirituality gave me some comfort and became central to my life. I prayed for Alice and searched for answers. I came to the conclusion that what had happened couldn't be explained in human terms. There were events in Alice's life which had damaged her, that was undeniable. She had been sensitive to Marty and my issues. Not only had she been badly bullied at primary school but at 16 years of age she had been raped by her first boyfriend. She suppressed and dissociated from these memories which emerged during her last year at school and were an undeniable trigger for what happened later. Even this, I felt, didn't explain the severity of her illness or account for her extreme behaviour. Looking back over her life I hadn't seen this coming, I couldn't see the signposts pointing the way to severe mental illness and suicidality. With my burgeoning spiritual awareness and inner wisdom I reached the conclusion that the answers could not be found in Alice's current life. There was more to it. This was soul stuff. Alice had brought in issues from other lifetimes, some unfinished business and she had chosen this lifetime to deal with it.

In a small way I had already observed the impact of past life trauma on my other two children. Could what Alice was experiencing be past life trauma of a more extreme kind? Why had this happened? Was there a higher purpose to this? I had been a committed and conscious parent, had tried so hard to make things perfect and now it had all blown up in my face. I thought of difficult children I had met over the years—how it had been easy to point the finger of blame at their parents and how readily I had done so. I couldn't relate to the stories from parents of rebellious and outrageous teenage behaviour. The previous year I had written a course for parents of teenagers and when I wrote the section on 'at risk teenagers' lamented the fact that I had no experience or understanding of this. I was smug; far too smug. Little did I know that soon I would be an expert on the subject!

As a child, Alice was loving, well behaved and dedicated to her family. Hugh and Mary were happy and well adjusted. As a teenager Alice become more anxious and shut down. She was close to me and we would talk about her life and as time went on her difficulties with friendships. When she was sixteen, my parenting books told me that it wasn't normal for a girl of this age to have such a close relationship with her mother, that teenagers needed the space to individuate and to find their own identity. Words like 'enmeshed' and 'co-dependent' leapt off the page and I realised it was important for Alice to take more responsibility for her own life. I started to discourage lengthy chats. It was at this time that she met her first boyfriend, the one who raped her. It was a downhill slide after that.

I had spent years doing everything humanly possible to create the perfect life for my children. Looking back it seemed the harder I tried the less perfect things became. I thought of some of the youth offenders I had met when running my Heart to Heart courses for teenage fathers in prison. Although I could tick the boxes of family dysfunction, poor education, no father figure and childhood abuse and neglect, for most of these youths, I realised they did not all fit this criteria or follow the same trajectory. A number of them had loving and responsible parents who were now heartbroken.

There was no 'one size fits all' for these teenagers. There were exceptions, there would always be exceptions and some situations that didn't make sense within the context of their current lifetime. Alice was one of these exceptions. Deep inside I knew that she had come in carrying baggage and I had agreed to help her. I started to see this situation in a wider context and had many questions. "Why had Alice chosen mental illness? Why had she chosen me to be her mother? Why had I agreed to become her mother? What was my contract with her? How was this situation part of a greater plan and a bigger picture? What was my learning in this?"I searched for answers and my questioning led me to the Akashic Records.

In the meantime Alice's new home had become, Ward 27, the adult psychiatric ward at Wellington Hospital. We visited her often and took her on outings. After a year she was even allowed the occasional night at home but as she was mostly still determined to end her life this was stressful and risky. She was not the sweet and compliant girl we had known, no longer loving and eager to please. She stopped eating and lost kilos in weight, was morose and sometimes unpleasant. Her hospital room was covered with black drawings of death, skeletons and horror. She wore the same blue hoodie for months, pulled down to hide her face. She was wracked with self-hatred which she usually directed at herself but was sometimes projected at the staff and at us. She kept instructions for her funeral in a folder in her room. She was tormented and her actions were extreme. She witnessed the behaviour of other patients in both the adolescent and adult psychiatric wards and started to act out in horrifying ways. As a child she had not thrown a single tantrum. She was making up for lost time now! Some of the staff found Alice a challenge but there were two—an experienced nurse named Carolyn and a psychologist, Gemma—who understood and cared about her and became her lifelines. I will always be grateful to them.

I adjusted to, but did not accept, this new situation and started looking for answers. Books I read were helpful. By this time Alice had been diagnosed with Borderline Personality Disorder (BPD), Depression, Anorexia and Post Traumatic Stress Disorder. I read widely about BPD and found that it is characterised by periods of intense and overwhelming emotions and impulsive behaviour. It is common for borderlines to relieve these feelings through self-harm.

The suicide rate for BPDs is high as the emotional pain can become so unbearable that death can seem like the only way out. These episodes of 'dysregulation' are very dangerous. During them the sufferer is highly vulnerable. For the first two years of her illness Alice was in this state for most of the time. Seven years later she still has these episodes but they are less frequent.

There are nine recognised symptoms of the illness and those with six or more of them are given the diagnosis. Alice displayed every symptom on the list in particular:

> » Identity disturbance—markedly and persistently unstable self-image or sense of self.

> » Impulsivity in at least two areas that are potentially self-damaging.

> » Recurrent suicidal behaviour, gestures, or threats, or self-mutilating behaviour.

> » Chronic feelings of emptiness.

I read spiritual books that gave me comfort and helped me to see and understand the workings of a greater, divine intelligence. A reading I had with Judith Prosser, a channel for the light, gave me some answers. I discovered that Alice had a soul history of suicide. She had not had many Earth lives and most of these had been traumatic. She had bailed out early in some of them and had set herself up for success in this lifetime but still had to face and overcome the challenges that had tripped her up previously. I was told that Alice was releasing deep soul trauma from a succession of very challenging lifetimes; that she had chosen this time to complete a number of soul cycles at once, that this was an ambitious task but that she would probably survive.

The plan was for her to come through this and live a long life but she had free will so would not necessarily make it. I was told that if she didn't, she would be welcomed and cared for on the other side. I had offered to be her mother for karmic reasons and because we had a close soul connection and I wanted to help her to heal and release her trauma. Being Alice's mother would also give me the opportunity to learn my chosen lessons and provide a springboard for me to fulfil my soul mission and to reach my potential. I was given a glimpse of future possibilities, of Alice as a mother, of Alice and I working together and told that I would find ways to lessen and clear some of the more extreme effects of her past life trauma.

Apart from this session with Judith, I soldiered on without professional help for two years. I was used to being the one others came to for help. It wasn't easy being on the receiving end. In early 2009, I attended my sister Judy's *Goddess Tara Retreat* in New Zealand's stunning Coromandel peninsula. I met some special people there and as we parted one of them pushed a phone number into my hand. She said, "If you feel you need some counselling, here is someone who can help you." An inner part of me yelled, "I am okay. I don't need help," but another part of me knew that I was supposed to contact Terri Morehu and that at the right time I would. Later that year, in the aftermath of Alice's ten days in intensive care following a near fatal overdose and much to the relief, I am sure, of my long-suffering friends, I got in touch with Terri and my work with her began.

Terri works in a unique way. She is a counsellor but one with channelling and clairvoyant abilities. She is gifted and beautiful. With her help I have been able to transform my life. She is expert at helping clients release inner-child hurt and in identifying limiting beliefs they have taken on in childhood and carried over from past incarnations. She can see the origins of these beliefs in other lifetimes and works with her clients to heal and release them. She was concerned before our very first session because as she prepared herself she had a vision of a man in uniform stooped over and stoking an oven in a concentration camp. She knew it was a picture of her next client and wondered how she was going to break the news that she had been a Nazi! Terri didn't need to worry. Her client, who was me, already knew. This information confirmed to me that Terri was a healer and a channel of the highest calibre and that I was meant to work with her.

In our very first session, Terri tuned in to Alice and saw her as a four year old girl in a hideous underworld dominated by a dark and controlling entity. Terri knew nothing about Alice or her situation but saw her as a small girl in chains, trapped, enslaved and controlled by evil. That night in a special session, Terri worked hard with the soul of Alice to release her from that dark place. I visited Alice a few days later and noticed a huge difference. The light had returned to her eyes. She was allowed a home visit and others noticed and commented on the change. The old Alice started to return in short bursts and we were delighted.

One day when Alice was four years old she went to play at the home of a friend. That night in the bath she told me that she had been sexually abused by the other girl. She put it in different words of course but I was horrified. She described what the other child had done to her and I knew it was not normal four year old behaviour. I told the girl's mother what had happened and it did not go down well. Alice was not the same after this incident. She became quieter and more anxious. I did my best to deal with it at the time but didn't see it as sexual abuse. To me this was something perpetrated by adults not a four year old playmate. In the light of subsequent events I now realise what a huge impact this had on my sensitive daughter and wish I had sought out an expert child counsellor. I considered this but part of me felt that if I made an issue of it, it would only get bigger and the person that I was then just wanted the whole thing to go away.

Terri told me that sexual violation is a gateway to dark energy and that this vibration had come into my daughter on that day. Once Alice became really unwell she spoke of a voice that urged her to harm herself and taunted and tormented her, telling her she was useless and evil and would be better off dead. She called this voice 'the Dictator.' Once Terri had worked to free Alice's soul this voice quietened down and was eventually silenced.

I worked with Terri on a regular basis. Now I had reached out for help there was much to do, particularly in healing **inner child** pain which had been triggered by Alice's illness. I became stronger inside and more committed to a spiritual path. Terri guided me to learn the lessons my soul had chosen as the mother of Alice.

> »   To be detached from outcome and that I have no control over anyone or anything.

> »   Not to 'rescue' others or take responsibility for their actions or emotions.

> »   To be independent of the good opinion of others (to not care what others think of me).

» To be humble, compassionate and non-judgmental.

» To love unconditionally.

» To trust in myself and in Spirit.

» To put my own needs first.

» To put boundaries in place with others.

» How to let go of fear.

» How to deal with unpredictable people and the most important one ...

» 'To let go and let God.'

It was a steep learning curve and one where the stakes have been high ... every day I have had to live with the fact that I could lose my daughter, but in the process I have been transformed and irrevocably changed for the better. My relationship with myself has improved. For someone who began her life mired in self-hatred and shame I now have deep love and respect for myself. In the many glimpses I have had into my past lives I have seen myself as an initiate in **Atlantis**, Greece and the Egyptian mystery schools. Like many lightworkers I believe I have been undergoing a twenty-first century version of the soul initiations of the past. It has been a rigorous process and one not for the faint hearted but I am emerging from the chaos. Along the way the personality self that was Chris Wilson has been healed and strengthened and now I am merging with my authentic self, my soul self and feel able to fully accept and embrace my mission in this lifetime.

Judith Prosser, Terri and my sister Judy had helped me fill in the gaps and make some sense of the ticking time bomb which imploded in my family but I wanted to know more. I had so many questions. A history graduate and former teacher, I had read about the Akashic Records, a reservoir of soul history, and was intrigued. I knew there must be a way to access them. I put out this thought.

One day while en route with Alice to a therapeutic community in the South Island of New Zealand we stopped in the town of Nelson. There is a spiritual book store there called *Possibilities*. I was drawn to that shop by an inner knowing that there was a book there I had to read. I saw it straight away. It was part of their window display, right in the middle so I couldn't miss it. *How to read your Akashic Records*, by Linda Howe. I read the book and taught myself Linda's technique for opening the Akashic Records. I accessed my own with interesting results.

I had trained in past life regression with Dolores Cannon and one day after regressing a friend, as an afterthought I decided to try out Linda Howe's method. It was nerve-racking and I had my eyes shut throughout but I spoke the words that came into my head as my client asked about her health issues and job prospects. My friend found this session helpful and over the next few months reported back as her life unfolded just as I suggested it would. I loved doing this work and started to give readings for others on a voluntary basis.

The feedback was gratifying. What I said resonated with people and things I told them started to happen. They began to see positive changes in their lives and I started to see the same in mine. Everything about my life improved—my health, career, relationships and my peace of mind. Every time I went into the Akashic Records for clients or myself I was benefitting from their healing energy. After three years of dealing with the intensity of Alice's illness and its fallout I was physically and emotionally exhausted. It had brought me to my knees. The high vibration and loving energy of the Akashic Records was exactly what I needed to heal and get back on my feet.

I practised hard, developing my own way of accessing the

Records, but had to be given a nudge by Terri to take the next step. With her urgings and the support of Donna, the friend who had given me Terri's phone number, I gave readings for strangers at the Christchurch 'Body Mind Spirit Festival.' Donna created my beautiful website which offered my services more widely and I have been working in the Akashic Records ever since with clients from all over the world.

Chapter 4
The Perfection of the Akashic Records

My Akashic Records idol is Edgar Cayce. He was a humble man who used his gifts to benefit others. I first heard of these soul records when I read about Cayce who lived in the USA from 1877 to 1945. Nicknamed, 'the sleeping prophet,' he was an unconscious trance channel who helped many clients with physical and emotional problems. He discovered his abilities as a young man when, after a severe bout of laryngitis, he was hypnotised and received information which he used to cure himself. He found he could help others in the same way, face-to-face and from a distance, and his fame spread.

He accessed the soul history of his clients through the Akashic Records and provided them with helpful information and guidance. He worked in a sleep state and could not remember any of the details. From 1923 Cayce's readings were recorded by his stenographer, Gladys Davis. Today there are 14,000 transcripts of Cayce's sessions preserved by the ARE (the Association for Research and Enlightenment) in Virginia Beach, Virginia, USA.

These days accessing the Records is a much simpler process. Luckily for me, going into a trance is no longer necessary. When I give a reading I open the Akashic Records by saying a prayer channelled from Spirit and then asking specific questions. The information comes to me in a sort of cosmic download. It doesn't come in a straightforward, linear way but in separate packets of light that somehow connect in my head and emerge from my mouth or onto the page in a coherent sentence. I have to keep writing or speaking or it stops the flow. When I work I try to link in with the guides of my client and am conscious of a group of souls in the Akashic Records who are helping me.

I ask clients to come with questions and issues they would like to explore. The Akashic Records are such a vast reserve of information that it helps to zero in on specific areas. As I go into the Records I usually get a picture of that person's soul history, where their soul originated, some of the challenges they have faced and their plan and mission. Sometimes an image from a significant lifetime flashes into my head. I am able to give some past life background to current relationships and difficulties and some direction for the future. Most of my clients ask about relationships, career, past lives, soul contracts and their life purpose and possibilities.

Every reading is different. In most readings I convey information, but in many I do healing work for example, clearing my client's energy field and facilitating the clearing and releasing of limiting beliefs. I also work with my clients and the higher selves of others alive and dead to heal soul trauma in individuals and groups, including families. I do what I am guided to do and work with my helpers in the Akashic Records and with the assistance of **Ascended Masters** and **Archangels**. I don't behave in any way that is unusual. My readings are conducted by phone, Skype or email. A face-to-face reading is often just a cosy, relaxed chat. The language I use is the normal, simple down-to-earth language I speak in my everyday life.

Email readings are different. Clients send me questions, I access their records and the answers write themselves. It is a form of channelling and the language is more formal. As I usually know nothing about the person I am reading for, a high level of trust is involved. This has been good training in getting my head out of the way and going with the flow of the information I receive.

It takes a leap of faith to do this work. All self-doubt and scepticism has to be put to one side and you simply have to trust. This was quite frightening at first. On a human level, this work brings with it huge responsibility. What I say is sometimes life changing for people and I want to get it right. I am always nervous when clients ask me what they should or shouldn't do when they are at an important cross roads in their life … should they leave their marriage, change jobs, move towns? I always emphasise that there are many possibilities and probabilities in the Records. Some events are pre-destined like who we will marry, and who will be our children for example.

There are certain signposts and events along the way but in the energy we are in now, the energy of the Fifth Dimension, very little is set in stone. Our lives are a blank canvas with the potential for us to be and to do anything that is in our hearts. In our Akashic Record there is information on possible future events and a blueprint for our life which we have collaborated with our guides and spiritual mentors to create—but we have free will and what is likely to occur will not necessarily happen. Just as in a football game, in life the ball often comes our way. It is up to us whether we choose to pick it up and run with it.

The idea that we create our reality through our beliefs is now widely accepted. If this is so anything we would like to happen is possible. Life is a work in progress and we can change the script moment by moment, thought by thought. If we want to change our lives we merely have to change our thoughts. In the new energy of the Fifth Dimension which is currently anchoring itself on Earth manifesting is easier and the gap between thought and creation is much smaller.

Earth is in the midst of a transformation. Since the **Harmonic Convergence** in 1987, light has been pouring in at an increasing rate. The slower moving energy of the Third Dimension with its dense vibration of fear and suffering is being replaced by a lighter and more loving energy. This process has been called **Ascension**. As I write this I am feeling the effects of the new energy and am integrating and assimilating it. This has always been the plan for our Third Dimensional planet.

This has been an intense time for humanity as we have undergone an extreme process of physical, emotional, mental and etheric clearing. For most of us it is a challenge to address the impact of our childhood experiences and the resulting physical and emotional ailments but what we have been doing and are still doing is dealing with beliefs and experiences we have carried through many human lifetimes. This is big stuff. Our 'slow progress' can make us feel frustrated and stuck.

In a soul context, against the backdrop of the hundreds and sometimes thousands of human lifetimes we have lived, our progress in this one lifetime has been phenomenal and our lives are not over yet! The good news is that as souls in the energy of the Fifth Dimension, we will have the opportunity to progress more rapidly. To do this we will have to be very careful what we think and conscious of our thoughts as they will continue to create our reality even faster than before.

Access to the Akashic Records has helped me put the traumatic events of the last few years in context and has helped me cope with and understand the intense personal process I and many here on Earth have been going through in the lead up to Ascension. As Judy Satori writes in *The Sunshine before the Dawn*, just over 100,000 years ago souls from higher dimensional places in our galaxy agreed to come to Earth and to live many cycles of lives in order to be here to assist at this time. These starseed souls had an additional purpose as they came to Earth to help activate a twelve-strand DNA potential within human beings. It is these strands that connect us to source, to our god-selves and to our star heritage. Over thousands of years this DNA template has become part of the DNA of all human beings. Through this we all have a connection to the stars and to this higher expression of ourselves. It was felt by the engineers of this experiment that humanity would have a greater chance of surviving and ascending to a higher dimension if all beings on Earth were wired in this way.

The energy that has been coming into the planet with increasing intensity over the last three decades is giving life to our DNA potential and has activated the cellular memory of people like me who have stellar soul origins. Many of my clients are starseeds and like me have experienced many consecutive lives on Earth. A number also come from the stars but have been able to return to their homes in other parts of the galaxy in between their human lifetimes. Some are experiencing their very first lives on Earth.

The 'Earth School' has not been an easy assignment. In his book, *Journey of Souls: Case Studies of life between lives*, Michael Newton, a hypnotherapist and pioneer in past life regression, confirms that life on Earth is the most challenging and exacting in the universe. His book contains transcripts of sessions with clients taken back to the moment of death and to the period in between their earthly lives. As they review their lives it is clear that each soul has a plan which interconnects and overlaps with the plans of those around them—that we all have our place and a special part to play. Our lives are divinely orchestrated to give us the opportunity for maximum soul growth and development. When we are facing adversity in life, on a soul level it is perfect.

If life on Earth can be so tough why do we choose to return here again and again? On this planet we have the opportunity for more rapid soul advancement. It is a place where we feel strong emotions that we have to learn to deal with: a place where we can more swiftly gain mastery. We face the challenge of living in a physical body and all that that entails but the soul rewards are great for a successful life on Earth.

Earth is a sensory place. As humans we have the ability to feel physical and emotional pain, to hear, to smell, to see, to touch and taste. Our greatest challenge is to master our emotions. Our sixth sense, the awareness of our spiritual nature and origins, is our least developed. As we are re-born into a human body what has been called 'the veil of forgetfulness' comes down taking away all conscious memories of past lifetimes, our plan for this lifetime and our soul origins. We are like the skipper of a yacht, with no GPS in a strange and stormy sea. It is as if we have been cut adrift and set up for failure. But we are not alone. Overlooking the whole process is a benevolent intelligence. Before each lifetime we are consulted and decide ourselves what situation will give us the greatest opportunity for soul growth. Much thought and careful planning goes into this. The balance must be right. An easy and happy life is wonderful from a human perspective but not so desirable on a soul level. What do we learn when life is easy? Not much. The steepest learning curve comes as a result of hardship and struggle.

Our lives are planned for many reasons but mostly so we can learn the lessons we feel we need to learn, address karma and unfinished business, be of service to humanity and progress as souls. We choose our parents and life situation carefully because it is these early years that lay the foundations for the life to come. We look at our goals, plan and mission for our coming lifetime and set ourselves up for success. Our birth circumstances, parents, siblings, extended family, intellect, physical appearance and characteristics and nationality are all carefully considered and chosen to fit in with our goals.

The soul information Michael Newton shares in his books, *Journey of Souls* and *Destiny of Souls*, confirms that a life time is not entered into without much planning and forethought. Every single aspect of the coming life and its possibilities are deliberated over at length. Souls are born into a situation that will give them the greatest chance to learn and master the lessons they have chosen. What seems flawed and imperfect in human terms is, on a soul level, perfect and for the highest good of those concerned. What makes no sense on a human level makes total sense in the light of the Akashic Records.

A couple came to me for a reading. The wife had had a slight disability when they married which had worsened over the years. She suffered from a variety of ailments from an autoimmune disorder and narcolepsy to a series of painful leg and hip fractures. She was unable to work and was highly dependent on her husband who worked to support her as well as completing most household tasks. As a young man he had been a free and adventurous spirit travelling the world and living life to the full. He told me of their meeting and how his mind kept coming up with all the logical reasons why he shouldn't pursue their relationship. She was eight years older and at the time came with an elderly grandmother who also needed care. Despite all this he felt committed to this woman whom he loved dearly.

During the reading I found that his wife, Sally was living her first lifetime on Earth. She had found it physically challenging and difficult to adjust. She had always felt like she didn't belong and was not fully present. She came from a far off place in our galaxy and before this lifetime had been a being of light. This explained her physical limitations. She was still learning to be in a body and the mechanics of this were a challenge. Her tendency to suddenly fall asleep was a way for her to stay in close contact with 'home.' I found that this was a pre-condition of her accepting her Earth contract and that, nervous about the other demands that this lifetime would present, she asked for a partner to support and assist her. The soul that was her husband, Colin, had agreed to take on this role. Her main goal in her current lifetime, I found, is to adjust to life on Earth and if this goes well the plan is she will return here in the future and make a more obvious contribution. As a soul Sally has much to offer. She has valuable knowledge and information to bring to Earth when the time is right and a close, telepathic connection to animals and birds. This lifetime is a precursor to her fully manifesting this.

There were several reasons why Colin had agreed to help Sally. He has a close soul connection with her from a time aeons ago when he too was a soul from the same star system. He is also a soul that has a history of raising his hand to help others but who has needed to learn the key importance of not enabling them in the process. He has an adventurous and experimental aspect which has often gotten him into trouble and which he has used in other lives to run away from and avoid responsibility. His current lifetime is teaching him what he feels he needs to learn. His wings have been clipped to give him the chance to learn the value of stability, security and to become more responsible, reliable and self-disciplined. His family are upstanding citizens which laid the groundwork for this life providing the conditioning to set himself up to fulfil his contract to Sally.

All is often not as it seems. We can find out why by exploring the Akashic Records. We have all observed relationships and behaviours that don't make sense. On a human level maybe, but on a soul level all is happening exactly as it is supposed to.

This learning has helped me cope with my own situation as the mother of Alice. Since Alice became ill the agony of the judgment of others and of my own self-judgment has been excruciating. Some people see a tormented young woman and jump to the conclusion that her life experiences and in particular the parenting she has received are responsible. Working in the Akashic Records has given me a more expanded view and I have come to see myself not as a villain or a victim but as a heroine. I have been chosen, and in fact have agreed, to help my daughter overcome human aspects that have been holding her back for a very long time. This is a selfless act of love. I deserve the highest accolades and so do all those who have taken on a similar soul assignment.

Over the years I have met many broken-hearted parents. I honour each and every one of them. Through my work in the Akashic Records and through personal experience I am learning not to take things at face value but to always know and trust in the bigger picture. On a soul level there are no mistakes. Our lives are painstakingly planned with our soul evolution and best interests in mind. The information I have discovered through my work in the Akashic Records has given me glimpses of a divine matrix and interdependence between souls and experiences that has astounded and delighted me. There is a purpose behind every single soul, every single lifetime and every single event. As human beings our experiences are interwoven and interleaved in a mystical, magical way that is nothing short of miraculous. This gift is a blessing. Through the Akashic Records I have come to see the beauty, harmony and perfection that is human life and for that I am profoundly grateful.

Chapter 5
Life Planning

Considerable planning goes into each human lifetime. While under hypnosis, Michael Newton's subjects told of the decision to reincarnate and the ensuing process. Newton speaks of the time between lives as a time of study and reflection. For most incoming souls a period of healing, rehabilitation and reorientation is needed. With their **spirit guides** they conduct a detailed review of the lifetime just completed. They evaluate what went according to plan and what didn't, the soul growth and learning that occurred and the pitfalls and missed opportunities.

Newton says when we die we are welcomed initially by souls we have known during our lifetime, but that we are closest to a small group of up to 20 who constitute our soul group. These souls have been with us almost since our soul's inception and have sometimes, but not always, been close to us in our immediate past life. Once we have spent time with the loved ones we recognise on a human level we join with these soul peers. This group along with our spirit guide assist us with the planning and preparation for our lifetimes.

Our guide is usually a being we have a close association with who has supported us throughout our recent incarnation. We have usually shared past lives, they may have been our guides before and there is a deep and enduring connection. Most of us have several guides. I have had clients with eight or more. Some of these are guides who come in at different times during our life span to help us with certain aspects of our learning and soul development. It is common to have a deceased family member, often a grandparent or great-grandparent, as a guide but we all have one main guide with the primary responsibility of overseeing our life and doing their best to help us keep to our plan.

It is a soul's choice to reincarnate, there is no coercion involved but some souls need a nudge if their soul mentors feel it would be in their best interests. Michael Newton, in his book, *Journey of Souls*, says that once the healing and rehabilitation from a lifetime is complete, we remember the pleasures of being human and yearn to once more become a physical manifestation of our soul.

When the wounds of a past life are healed and we are again totally at one with ourselves we feel the pull of having a physical expression for our identity.

Journey of Souls, Michael Newton pp 201-202

It is possible to remain in a soul state indefinitely if that is our choice but the Earth school offers a faster track to evolution and spiritual growth by comparison. I believe that souls choose to return mainly for this reason and to:

» Address karma.

» Complete unfinished business.

» Help out at a crucial time in Earth's evolution.

» Assist other souls on their journey.

Karma is a residue that is created as a result of every soul action and interaction. A key reason for choosing to reincarnate is so we can repay the karmic debt we feel we owe. It is not mandatory that we do this. We are not forced into repaying karma. Like our decision to reincarnate, atoning for past life actions we regret is entirely up to us. Many of us make this choice and have specific contracts with others which are designed to clear karma.

The karmic relationship is the challenging one where we see ourselves behaving badly and are not sure why. We come back time and time again to work on these difficult relationships, hoping to heal past rifts and balance the scales so we can move on and be free. The problem is that after repeating unhealthy patterns over many lifetimes these behaviours can be so entrenched it is easy to get sucked back into a vortex of disharmony. Most of us have a karmic relationship with someone. Against our better judgment we feel irresistibly drawn to a person or that person is a part of our extended family and a thorn in our side. If we have a history of past life mistreatment of another soul, a new life gives us the opportunity to do things differently and to heal the relationship. Once this has happened any future lifetimes spent together will be through choice not obligation.

A single mother asked me about the relationship with her son's father. I found that their relationship was karmic and designed to help them learn chosen lessons.

You have been with this man before and he has never treated you well. He has taken advantage of you in many lifetimes and harmed you both emotionally and physically. You were husband and wife in a lifetime in the Middle East. You were older than your husband and the marriage was arranged. You loved him deeply. He had some emotional issues and you helped him with these. With your love and support he became a man of standing in the community. You gave him everything you had and propped him up for years.

Unfortunately, you were unable to give him the one thing he most wanted—a child. He found another wife and divorced and banished you. You were displaced and homeless. Your family was ashamed of you and rejected you as well. You had

no status within the narrow confines of your society and were
forced to live on the streets and beg for food. You died alone
and miserable.

Both my client and her ex-partner have chosen to address karma in this lifetime and to learn the importance of giving and receiving love in a balanced way. Their relationship has been perfect for this.

Sunita, a young and beautiful Indian woman wanted some background on her relationship with her sister-in-law, Anjali. Sunita had always mistrusted Anjali, finding her controlling and unpleasant. She had been close to her brother before his marriage but felt his wife had come between them.

Through accessing Sunita's Akashic Record I found that in another lifetime, Sunita had been Angali's daughter-in-law. She was the fourth and last wife of Anjali's middle aged son who was besotted with her. Sunita did not love her husband and married him only because of pressure from her family who saw this as a step up the social ladder. Sunita was young and wilful and her mother-in-law was old and tired. Her husband adored his new wife and spent more time with Sunita than he did with his mother and other wives put together. His aging mother resented the attention her new daughter-in-law received. Her life had been calm and peaceful before her son's marriage to Sunita and now the dynamics had changed. She felt she had not only lost her son but also her power and control in the household. She wanted Sunita out of the way and decided to poison her. She did so slowly so no one would suspect by putting small amounts of a noxious herb into her daughter-in-law's food.

With the help of the Akashic Records I found that Sunita's brother in this lifetime had been her husband in this past life and that Sunita and Anjali had come back together to give their relationship another chance. Anjali wanted to atone for the past life murder of her sister-in-law. On a subconscious level they both held memories from the past and this was causing problems in the relationship as they automatically lapsed into old behaviours. Feelings of jealousy and mistrust were triggered particularly when they were around Sunita's brother. Her reading helped Sunita see this relationship differently and it has improved.

This same client also has a karmic relationship with her husband, Alistair, who she is strongly committed to but is not sure why. She says she ' feels like she is giving a great deal for not much in return.' I found that in another life Sunita had been Alistair's husband. She was a travelling merchant who put his own needs and those of others before his duty to his wife. When the merchant's wife (Alistair) died suddenly and unexpectedly he (Sunita) was filled with remorse and wanted the chance in this lifetime to support and care for (Alistair) in a way she didn't in their earlier lifetime together.

Karma can have a twist as we often choose lives or experiences that have a direct link with our last lifetime, offer us opportunities to make amends and help us to see things from an opposite perspective.

Terumi, a Japanese friend who grew up in the shadow of Hiroshima and Nagasaki, was horrified when I discovered she had been a US Army pilot who was part of the group involved in planning the dropping of atomic bombs on that country in 1945. She was shocked at this revelation but admitted it resonated with her particularly as she has always had a fascination with the USA and World War II aircraft.

I myself, have noticed many karmic aspects to my life. When I delivered my parenting courses to inmates in our local men's prison the high fences and barbed wire were familiar to me—I felt comfortable right from the start. I hope I have managed to help the prisoners in a way that I wasn't able to in my last life. I ended that lifetime in Germany with no desire or will to live, as my desperate family tried unsuccessfully to reach me. This time round I have chosen to be on the receiving end and have suffered as the mother of Alice, who we had difficulty connecting with during her darkest days. Alice's immediate past life ended in Auschwitz and part of my chosen karma is to help her recover from the trauma which is still affecting her. As a German soldier I wanted desperately to help victims of the Third Reich and now one lifetime later I am getting my chance. Part of my soul contract with my daughter is to help her in ways I haven't managed to in past lives.

Many souls, myself included, choose to come back to complete unfinished business. In answering a client's questions, "Why are my two daughters in my life? What is our soul connection?" I received the following:

You have chosen this relationship as you greatly regret making what you feel was a wrong choice in your most recent lifetime together. You were their mother in Poland during World War II. You knew they were in danger of being rounded up by soldiers but left them for a few hours to get food. It was a tough call but you were facing starvation. You told them to hide but the soldiers came, found your children and took them away. That was the last you saw of them and you lost the will to live. You were captured and sent to a concentration camp where you died feeling guilty and bitterly regretting the decision you made that day.

It is a common soul theme to want to reconnect with those with whom a relationship has ended in a sudden and traumatic way. Sometimes there is a karmic aspect to this but more often than not it is seen as a chance for completion and is an extension of the eternal love and connection between souls.

I have an increasing number of clients who are new to the earth plane or who have had a few lifetimes here but in earthly terms are relatively inexperienced. They have been existing in other worlds and star systems but have made the soul choice to come to Earth to assist humanity in this crucial time of change. These souls are fortunate as they don't come in with the baggage carried by most of us. The down side is that their lives can be challenging. Their true home is a place where the dense vibration of fear doesn't exist. It is difficult for them to understand human behaviour, to cope with the negativity and to adjust to the lower vibration of Earth.

These souls are highly sensitive with a subconscious memory of a different kind of existence and they often struggle and feel out of place and unhappy. They have been arriving in large numbers during the last twenty years—first as the so-called Crystal and, more recently, the **Rainbow Children**. The **Crystal Children** have lived on Earth before but carry no karma and have been thoroughly prepared for their mission. The Rainbow Children are new to planet Earth but have also been well prepared in advance. They choose parents who will understand and support them and not shut them down. They are starting to feel more comfortable in the higher vibrational Fifth Dimensional energy that has been coming to Earth in increasing waves in recent years.

There are a few souls who are living their first lifetime here but were born a generation or two earlier than these children. They are the pioneers, the scouts who have been sent ahead to pave the way. They are brave and adventurous and their journey has been difficult. I gave a reading to one such soul. She was so shocked by the positive light the Akashic Records shed on her that she rejected my words at first. Her life has been tough and she feels a failure on every level as a mother, a wife and a human being. Her Akashic Record told a completely different story. I learned that my client, Iona, had agreed to come to Earth on a special assignment to help carry and transmute fear from the collective consciousness of humanity. A first lifetime on Earth is challenging enough but her extreme sensitivity to Earth's lower vibrations made things even more difficult. She lacked confidence and was anxious—which was not surprising as she had been carrying the fears and insecurities of others as well as her own.

You are able to hold and transmute fear from the collective consciousness of humanity. This is a specialised job which has been needed in your lifetime to prepare Earth for Ascension. You have pulled the darkness of humanity through your physical body and released and transmuted it to a higher vibration.

You had the choice to come in later as one of the new, evolved children but chose to come early as a pioneer and a way shower. You are a courageous soul and are esteemed very highly by the Galactic Council who have been doing all they can to assist you with your work.

In reply to Iona's question, "Why have I not recognised my true potential and what do I need to do to make it happen?" I got the following:

*In the eyes of the **Galactic Council** and according to your pre-life plan, you have realised your potential, have conscientiously been of service to mankind and fulfilled your mission. Looking at your life through human eyes this may not seem to be the case. If you choose, there is much you can do in the rest of this lifetime to smooth the way and assist the **Star Children** who have been coming into the planet in recent years. Your contribution to humanity has been outstanding. You have done this work in the way only you (because of your unique soul heritage) have been able to. As we move more fully into the Fifth Dimension you will feel more at home on Earth and your life will become happier and easier.*

The email from Iona of disbelief and denial was followed by one several days later which was more positive and I could see she was starting to recognise her true self. She is now releasing her own fear and the fear she has carried for others and has stepped firmly onto a spiritual path. She has begun reaching out to those with intergalactic but not similar origins (Iona's soul heritage is rare) and is beginning to enjoy life.

One of the main reasons we choose human life is to help others. Written into our soul contracts are clauses outlining the ways we intend to assist other souls on their journey. A chance meeting, a lifelong arrangement, these soul agreements have one main purpose, to support others to do what they have come to do. After the way things went 'pear shaped' at the end of my last life I wanted support at the beginning of this one. I was frightened to come in alone and the soul that is my twin sister Jenny stepped up to the task. She has always been there for me and I do my best to reciprocate.

Elise asked me about her soul contract with her friend Kelvin. I found they had very different approaches to life and complementary strengths which they had agreed to share to help each other to reach their goals.

Kelvin is here to give you the support and confidence to move forward and you are here to show him a calmer and gentler way of approaching life and the importance of patience, trust and fortitude. He has agreed to help you to believe in yourself and to show you how to translate and create the vision you have for your future into reality. You have a contract to help him smooth off some of the more impulsive aspects of his character and to teach him the beauty and power of being and trusting.

Kelvin and Elise have different ways of chasing their dreams. Kelvin is a man of action while Elise draws on an inner well of strength and inspiration. They have agreed to teach each other the importance of combining the two.

Kelvin is here to help and to show you how to translate and create the vision you have for the future. He will teach you about taking small, practical action steps and you will show him how a balance of action and inaction is needed to manifest. You agreed to teach him that an important part of the creation process is going inward and getting into the right space energetically, emotionally and mentally. Doing all we can to force things to happen is not enough. All must be aligned in mind, body and spirit.

Like the seasons, life goes in cycles. When nothing much is happening in the outer world, there is always a great deal happening on the inner, and strong foundations are being laid down for the future. This is just as important a part of the manifestation process as ticking off your 'to do' list.

Your contract is to teach Kelvin about the power of being and his is to teach you about the importance of doing.

On a soul level, Elise and Kelvin have agreed to support each other to make their dreams a reality. They may be coming at it from different directions but the plan is that by helping each other they will end up in the same place.

The 'big picture' is that you will both learn how to live following your hearts and intuition.

Once a soul decides to be reborn our support networks are spurred into action. Michael Newton discusses how we decide on the circumstances of our next life with the support of our soul group, our guide and a body called the '**Council of Elders.**' After a thorough study of our immediate past life and taking into account other aspects and experiences of our soul journey throughout time, we decide on:

Our goals for our next life.

» The lessons we would like to learn.

»   What karma we would like to address.

»   Our life purpose and mission.

Our goals and life lessons are often those that seem simple on the surface but are far from it, for example:

Learning to:

»   Love and look after ourselves.

»   Speak our truth.

»   Be patient.

»   Be self-disciplined.

»   Give to others without expectation of anything in return.

»   Detach from unhealthy relationships.

»   Deal with anger.

»   Overcome addictions.

If we have a soul history of dominating and controlling others, of being a victim or of taking on too much responsibility, we may choose life circumstances that force us to face these challenges head on. We may decide to have domineering or overly responsible parents for example. We can choose to face human aspects that our soul wishes to bring into balance and heal or to strengthen certain qualities (such as patience, unconditional love, compassion or humility). We may decide to focus on just one life lesson, especially if it is a lesson we have been attempting to master over many lifetimes. More advanced souls often choose more.

Laura is a young Australian wife and mother who has already

faced much hardship. She has chosen to have a rocky start to life and to learn her lessons in a concentrated and intense way while she is young to help her to become a strong woman and healer in service to others. She asked about her life lessons and I received this information:

The key lessons you are here to learn are:

> » *Patience and that good things come to those who wait.*

> » *To love and accept yourself unconditionally.*

> » *Self-respect. To value yourself and not accept abusive and thoughtless treatment from others.*

> » *That you are perfect as you are and do not need to be supported or propped up by anyone or anything.*

> » *You are strong and powerful and have all your own answers.*

Your life purpose is to reconnect with the divine feminine aspects of your soul self and to become a powerful woman: an avatar and emissary of light and love. Through your own life challenges and lessons you will learn much to help others who have faced similar trials. The plan is for you to fully embrace your god-self and to help others to find their own light within.

Our human relationships, and particularly our intimate ones often provide the backdrop for our major life lessons. Mollie has chosen to work on her main lesson for this lifetime,' the appropriate use of power and control,' through her relationships with men. This has been a thread that has run through many of her lives. I told Mollie:

You have had difficulty getting the balance right. You have either let circumstances or others control you or you have swung the other way and out of fear been too rigid and controlling.

In her current life, relationships she has had with four partners, Harry, Tom, Zach and Morris have highlighted this issue. She asked about these.

Harry:

He has been in your life before and broke your heart in a lifetime in France where he went off to war and never came back. You planned a short reunion in this life to heal that pain from the past and the anxiety around separation. In this French life you had no control over what happened or the outcome. You wanted to come back together so you could feel more in control of the situation.

One day you were happily betrothed to Harry and dreaming of your future together and the next he was gone. You waited the rest of your life for him to return and he never did. This was heartbreaking for you and you lost your power after this.

This experience ground you down. You became disillusioned with life and it brought up huge anger and mistrust which you have carried ever since. It has given you a fear of being controlled and of losing control, particularly in relationships and is one of the reasons why you have struggled to have long lasting and healthy relationships.

Being back with Harry helped bring these old feelings to the surface so they could be released.

Tom:

This was also a relationship to help you learn about control. The lifetime with Harry was about dealing with or facing circumstances beyond your control and this relationship was about learning what it is like to be controlled.

You have had a life with Tom before. The reason you came back together again was so you could have the opportunity to repay a karmic debt. You were his wife in a lifetime long ago. He was much older and you did not want to marry him but did so to please and obey your father. You were young and had no idea what marriage entailed.

Sex with this man disgusted you and you resisted it. He raped you repeatedly and treated you cruelly. You felt trapped, especially when you started to have children. Leaving wasn't an option in those days. You loved your children and would not leave them so you killed your husband in a way that couldn't be detected.

Coming back together has given you the opportunity to end the relationship in a more civilised way and has also given you the chance, by moving to a place of forgiveness in this life, to heal the past. Tom still has a controlling nature and it was important for you to learn that in the twenty-first century you have the power to leave any situation that is not making you happy.

Zach:

This relationship was about you being the one in control and learning to use your power wisely. In this relationship you were the one calling the shots. It was still not healthy as you went too far the other way.

Morris:

The lesson here was also about control. You were attached to outcome in this relationship. You had a direction you wanted it to take and knew how you wanted things to turn out. You did everything you could to make this happen but it was not enough. It was a chance for you to learn the importance of letting go of control and that we have no control over outcome or how people choose to act and behave.

As usual these experiences, as painful as they were on a human level were perfect for Molly's goals in this lifetime.

In this lifetime the plan is for you to learn that the best relationships are those where the power is shared and there is mutual love, trust and respect. Your relationships with these men have been a gift and have helped you to learn about yourself and what is right for you. By experiencing what you don't want, you will now be able to create what you do want—a loving and equal partnership.

Once we have identified our lessons for the life to come we look at the karma we would like to address and our mission and overall life purpose. Often the repayment of karma will fit in with our chosen lessons.

A male client loves his wife and family and has a strong sense of commitment to them but finds the responsibilities of being a husband and father daunting at times. His reading revealed past lives of adventure and of pitting himself against the elements. I saw him as a sailor with Christopher Columbus, an explorer in the Arctic Circle and a soul who has often lived a nomadic and solitary life. In this lifetime he has a love of travel and adventure but because of financial constraints and family responsibilities he has been unable to satisfy these urges. Being in a long term relationship with a wife and a family to support has restricted him but has given him the opportunity to repay karma (he has abandoned his wife in previous lives) and to learn his life lessons.

This time round he has chosen to learn about responsibility and the joy of connecting with and being loved by others. He has resisted his situation at times and has sometimes considered escape but he knows deep down this is not an option if he is to stick to his life contract. The fact that he chose to be born into a family where his father and other male forebears have been faithful to their partners and where his father was an alcoholic is no mistake. His father's drinking made this client overly responsible as a child, bringing this central theme into his life at a young age. Part of his life purpose is to learn when and when not to be responsible and to bring this human characteristic into balance.

In between lifetimes we receive help to prepare for our next incarnation. As mentioned previously, there is no compulsion or pressure to reincarnate, the decision is entirely up to us. It is usually made because life in a human body provides a unique opportunity for us to learn our chosen lessons. Once we give the green light there is a rallying of forces and we are supported to organise life circumstances which will maximise the potential for soul development and growth.

With each new lifetime comes the precious opportunity to overcome the challenges and human flaws which have hampered our soul progress and to move closer to the god within.

Chapter 6
Soul Contracts

With our support team we carefully consider all aspects of our next life, particularly our physical body, genetics, geographical location, socio-economic situation and who will be our parents, siblings and children.

One of my clients has chosen physical disability to help learn life lessons of patience and perseverance. She has also agreed to help her mother repay karma from a lifetime when the two of them were soldiers and she left her to die on a battlefield. Her mother has asked for the opportunity to help care for her in a way she was unable to then. Another reason for her life choice is that this physically challenging lifetime will speed up her evolution.

We search for the best available opportunities in the body and select the optimum childhood circumstances to get us on track to fulfilling our soul mission and purpose.

In my own situation I have learned that the soul that is my daughter Alice has taken her life before and is hoping to break this pattern. She considered the circumstances of her current lifetime carefully so it would not only provide the ingredients for what would unfold but also set her up for success. Souls who commit suicide need to return to face the same challenges if they are to continue to evolve. I know that a great deal of planning went into this lifetime of Alice's. She has extraordinary support in the spirit realms with eight spirit guides, one of whom is Archangel Michael. She also has a high pain threshold and internal organs (her liver in particular) which are robust and strong. She is getting huge assistance to overcome the hurdles that have defeated her in the past but this does not mean that she will make it to the end of the race. She has always had a strong, determined streak and my money's on her but it won't necessarily happen.

One thing that is unique about life on Earth is that we are given free will. The choices we make and whether we stick to our contracts and plan for our life are up to us. We are on a journey we can't remember beginning. Along the way we have forgotten where we are going and why. Is it any wonder that so many of us get lost? We have support, and in some cases huge support, but most of us aren't aware of it. Our guides certainly look out for us and try to impress in our minds thoughts and advice which will keep us on track but there is a universal law that governs their actions which states that they cannot violate our free will and can only help us if we ask. We are spiritual beings living a human experience but are not consciously aware of it. Many of us feel as if we are from an alien planet (in many cases we are!), don't feel comfortable here and carry a subconscious yearning for home. We have no human remembrance of our goals, life plan or contracts. Under these circumstances it is amazing how successful most of us are.

Why aren't we born knowing the details of our soul history and heritage? For those who have lived many lifetimes it is thought it would stop us from fully experiencing our current lives and that it is better for us to start out with a clean slate. I have one client who has vivid past life recall and for him this has proved a curse not a blessing. He has had a difficult adult life constantly remembering and re-living past life trauma. He has been killed in many lifetimes and the resulting fear, intense emotions and karmic miasma have left him in a state of paralysis at times.

With the help of our guides we draw up soul contracts with the individuals who will share our upcoming lifetime and a contract with the **spiritual hierarchy** which encapsulates our goals for the life to come, our life purpose and overriding mission. Our soul contracts with others are unique to the situations and individuals involved. They take into account any karma and ways in which we plan to help others with their chosen lessons and in creating the highest vision for their life. Contracts with those we will have a close lifetime connection with such as family members can be detailed while others (for example a stranger who changes a flat tyre for us) are short and to the point.

We know we are keeping to our contract when we feel compelled to say something to someone, to help them in a certain way and as if we are living and speaking from our hearts. At these moments it is as if time stops and we are touched by grace. What we are doing or saying may not be logical and may seem out of character but it feels right. If we stop and listen we can almost hear the celebration in the realms of spirit. There is much rejoicing when we stick to the terms of our contracts. If we tune in to our inner voice and look for the signs it is easy to know when we are following our plan and getting the thumbs up.

Sue, a middle aged woman with many spiritual gifts and abilities, has a soul history of being persecuted for her beliefs and practices. She has been burnt as a witch, tortured during the Spanish Inquisition and has suffered greatly. In this lifetime she has suppressed her healing abilities because of a deep fear of this happening again. I discovered that she carries the belief, 'When I step out and am different I suffer.' She has not had an easy relationship with her husband who has watched on in several lives while she has been unjustly treated and killed. He has asked to be her husband in order to repay karmic debt but subconscious memories from the past have at times triggered old patterns between them. For Sue the relationship has brought up self-doubt and a feeling of mistrust and for her husband has triggered scepticism and a tendency to give greater credence to the views of others.

Here is Sue's contract with her husband:

> *This relationship is perfect for you both to learn your chosen lessons in this lifetime. Your lessons are around self-belief and self-acceptance and you have agreed to:*

> » *Learn to speak your truth to your husband with love.*

> » *Show him that all works out when one is following their heart and their highest purpose.*

> » *Teach him to let go of fear, particularly that related to security and the unknown, and to trust.*

> » *Lead your husband and family into the new energies and show them a higher way of living and being.*

> » *Be compassionate, non-judgmental and uncon-ditionally loving but to stand in your own power and put up boundaries when necessary.*

A young woman named Marie, asked me for details of her contracts with family members. A large and close family, she had a strong sense of being with them before. I found that this family group had been together during many lifetimes in different configurations. One of the strengths of Marie's family is the close connection between the women. Her mother, Anne, and three sisters are all highly evolved and have special and unique talents to offer at this time on Earth.

Marie has a soul history of self-doubt which has meant that her remarkable personal qualities and gifts have often been underutilised. Upon accessing Marie's Akashic Record I linked in with her soul essence which was pure, untainted and special.

You have an open heart and a way of relating to people which opens them up and helps them to see the best in themselves and to be their best. You have a soft and gentle energy which is loving, compassionate and healing and has a positive impact on all you come in contact with.

I found that over time Marie has come to doubt her own truth and has considered it safer to follow the mainstream ideology of whatever culture she has been a part of.

I see you living in communist Russia. You went along with the totalitarian belief system because it was safer even though in your heart you questioned it and did not believe in the way the society was engineered and operated.

You numbed yourself to your inner pain and to the pain that you witnessed around you because of experiences in previous lives where you learned it was dangerous to be different and to speak up.

This life is about you learning to follow your inner voice and to live your truth. It is also about reclaiming your power and not hanging back or being second best. You have many unique abilities, in particular as a teacher and a writer. If you reconnect with your magnificent soul self and don't allow self-doubt or the needs of others to hold you back you will reach your potential.

Marie asked for the details of her soul contracts with one of her sisters, Emma, who is a published author of psycho-spiritual books, and her parents. The contracts (below) show the way in which souls work together to help others to fulfil their destiny.

Soul contract with Emma:

» *To love and support each other.*

> » *To support her in every way you can as and when she needs it.*

> » *To gain strength from her guidance and encouragement but to stand in your own energy and speak your own truth.*

Emma's contract with you is to show you what is possible and to support you to step into your power and abilities and to reach your potential.

Marie's contract with her mother, Anne, revealed that they have chosen to be together to complete unfinished business and to give each other love and support. It also confirms that on a higher level, Marie's chosen family fitted perfectly with her plan and goals for this lifetime.

Soul Contract with Anne:

> » *To love her and to be a soothing and healing energy in her life.*

> » *To help her to see the goodness in herself and others. You have been together before and have a strong and loving connection. Your last life together was cut short when Anne, who was again your mother, died of consumption. You were the only daughter of Irish peasants and you loved and nursed your mother. (I can see you lovingly and patiently dabbing her forehead with a cloth). As souls you decided you wanted the chance to be together again and to live out adult lives as mother and daughter. Your mother (Anne) wanted the chance to be the mother she couldn't be in that Irish lifetime. The family composition and dynamics*

this time round are also perfect for your soul plan for this lifetime and for your growth.

Marie's soul contract with her father, Michael, gave details of what she had agreed to teach him and showed that an important purpose of their relationship was to give her father the opportunity to balance karma.

Soul Contract with Michael:

» *To love and accept him as he is.*

» *To help open his heart and to teach him about love, acceptance and forgiveness.*

» *To show him that gentleness, compassion and vulnerability are a strength.*

» *To give him the opportunity to repay a karmic debt as he was once one of your persecutors. In that lifetime he was a wealthy farmer of some influence in your community. You were educated and intelligent and started to get a following for your Protestant,(Calvinist) beliefs. You weren't into power but he resented your growing influence in a village where he saw himself as a leader. He was threatened by your knowledge and education and he denounced you and had you driven away.*

You became an outcast and were forced to leave the people you loved and to never return. This reinforced your belief that it is better and safer to go along with the belief of the majority and not to stick your neck out. You have been playing this out ever since.

The most detailed contracts are often those between parents and their children. I don't open the Akashic Records of children but have found that I can get information about their soul path and life purpose by going into their parents' Records. Belinda, the mother of three young children, asked me about the contract with her eldest child, Sam. He was giving her increasing cause for concern because he had become very clingy, getting upset when she left him at his preschool. At only four years old he was becoming increasingly anxious and haunted by fears which seemed irrational to her. I found that Sam was a very sensitive and special boy and that on a soul level there were good reasons for his behaviour:

Sam has not had many Earth lives and the ones he has had have ended in a traumatic way. He is much more comfortable in other parts of the galaxy that have a higher and more loving vibration than Earth. He has chosen to come here at this time in an effort to complete his mission.

He chose his parents carefully. As his parents you are both at a soul level where you can understand him and give him what he needs—open minded parents with little karma and baggage and a loving and stable home. His experiences on Earth have been very difficult. He has ended up alone and misunderstood and has been punished, tortured and even killed for being different.

Belinda's contract with Sam:

» *To love, nurture and respect him.*

» *To help him to feel safe in the world after many lifetimes of not feeling or being safe.*

» *To provide a stable upbringing.*

» *To reflect back his uniqueness and inner beauty.*

» *To love and accept him just as he is. To recognise his special needs and to do your best to meet these.*

» *To be a refuge of love and understanding he can turn to when the harshness of the outside world becomes too much.*

» *To help him adapt, adjust to and thrive on Earth.*

» *To help him deal with his fears of disaster, of people and of life itself.*

» *To support him to use his gifts to fulfil his mission which is to become a powerful and important teacher in the New Earth.*

» *To be there for him throughout his life because in another lifetime as his mother you died in childbirth and left him as a young boy. He missed you terribly and remembers losing all the security and happiness he had in that lifetime after your death.*

This information resonated with Belinda. Knowing about Sam's past lives and her soul contract with him helped her understand the deeper reasons for her son's behaviour and they were both much happier.

In Belinda's words:

My relationship with Sam has transformed and his energy feels calmer. He is communicating his feelings articulately and specifically rather than them bursting out of him angrily or physically. He is full of hugs and kisses for everyone and seems to be exploding with excitement and happiness.

My energy and thoughts shifted greatly after the reading, and I realise now the degree to which these affect him.

Soul contracts are sacred covenants which nail down the ways we can help each other individually and collectively during our time on Earth. Much thought is given to the terms of these contracts and interwoven through them are karmic and other considerations. Whether we choose to follow or not to follow the terms of our contracts we feel it in our heart, mind and soul. We have no conscious memory of them but soul contracts are etheric backdrops to our lives which greatly influence the way we choose to live them. They are in essence, a reflection of the underlying purpose of human life which is to help each other to grow and evolve.

Chapter 7
Soul Potential and Life Purpose

Many clients ask me what they can do to realise their soul potential. It is easy to talk about this because as soon as I go into someone's Akashic Record I am surrounded by it. I enter a vast, cavernous space filled with wisdom and possibilities, an enormous cave glittering with glow worms of hope and carrying an ancient and sacred vibration. The potential of each soul is like a gigantic subterranean village with many chambers and tunnels. I stand in this space, link in with the spirit of whoever I am working with and am filled with awe. During a reading I believe that my words carry the vibration of the potential of that soul, act as an intermediary between Heaven and Earth and give my clients a glimpse of their own magnificence. Being able to hold up a mirror so they can see themselves at their best is what I love most about my work.

For every life ever lived there is a purpose and every individual living soul has a mission to accomplish. This idea of a soul mission is especially relevant to souls choosing to incarnate on the Earth at this time. It is a unique moment in history. We have just completed a fourth consecutive period of 26,000 years and a larger cycle of time of 104,000 years. On 21 December 2012 what is called the '**Shift of the Ages**' occurred when the Earth aligned with the galactic core of the Milky Way and crystalline solar light flowed onto the planet birthing us into the Fifth Dimension. According to teacher, Patricia Cota-Robles, in her January 2013 newsletter this shift happens once in a million years and is offering great opportunities from a soul and human perspective for those in a human body. This unique blend of Third and Fifth Dimensional energy is triggering intense experiences that are helping us let go of the past and ushering in a fresh wave which will help us manifest our dreams and reach our potential.

Those of us currently living on Earth have an unprecedented opportunity to live the dream, to merge with our authentic soul selves and be all that we can be. As well as those who have been weighed down by the constrictions of the Third Dimension there are many souls who have lived either a few or no Earth lives who are here to help at this crucial moment in our history. We know deep down that if we truly want to reach our potential the time is now.

So what is holding us back from being the best version of ourselves? For many of us it is the lead weight of negative past life experiences that drags us down in lifetime after lifetime. Most of us start out swimming strongly and skimming across the waves, then life gets in the way, old trauma is activated and we see ourselves as 'not good enough.' The following information I received for a client, speaks to many of us:

> *You are on track to recognise and claim your true potential. Do not worry or chastise yourself because in your eyes all is not happening fast enough. In the context of the many lifetimes you have had, all is on track and perfect. You came to Earth from the stars and chose to experience every facet of the human experience. You have done this and not surprisingly along the way have accumulated some dross in the form of limiting beliefs, karma and past life experiences. These need to be healed and released before you can fully step into your power and soul essence. You are on track to do this. You may look at your life and feel that in a human context you have made little progress.*

Rest assured that you have been doing necessary inner work and are advancing rapidly on a soul level. You have needed to purify yourself and to release and heal on many levels before you can reach your potential.

And in another case:

You have been held back by limiting beliefs you have taken on in this and many previous incarnations. Progress in the Third Dimensional energy has seemed slow and difficult. You have lived hundreds of lifetimes since you first incarnated on Earth as a starseed.

You came because you understood the crucial importance to the Earth and the Universe, of bringing in light and assisting human beings to activate their twelve-strand DNA potential during Earth's Ascension process.

This lifetime is the culmination of all your soul experiences and the wisdom you have amassed. It is time now to access this to help humanity

As part of the preparation for the work you are here to do you have been undergoing some deep karmic cleansing. This has been challenging and you have felt as if you have been making no progress and at times as if you are regressing and sabotaging yourself. This has all been necessary to clear the way for the future.

This process is nearly at an end. The new energy that is coming in is activating the memory of who you really are. You have guides around you who are waiting to work with you and who are gently reminding you of your soul heritage.

The following client has a more recent star ancestry. In this incarnation she chose to have a physical infirmity as a child which restricted her and triggered memories and beliefs from other human lifetimes which are still stopping her from reaching her potential.

Your thoughts limit you. This lifetime has been challenging for you. You have at times felt trapped and limited in your body and this has translated to your thinking. You have taken on beliefs of limitation and self-doubt and these have held you back. It has been a while since you lived on Earth in a human body. Before coming into this lifetime you returned to your star of origin and worked to refine healing and other techniques which you will (in time) introduce to Earth.

Your previous lives have had their challenges and as soon as you were born in this lifetime and were back in a human body many of these old feelings and beliefs flooded back. It is time now to leave these behind and to embrace your soul magnificence. There is still some fine-tuning to do with the human part of you which sees life on Earth as limited and limiting.

Before this incarnation you had many powers and capabilities. Your challenge in this lifetime is to remember this, accept it and believe that you can bring these talents and abilities to Earth. It is time to start to see yourself as you really are, a being of light with wisdom, knowledge and skills you have brought from your true home and can use to help others.

A recurring message for many clients who ask what they need to do to reach their potential is to believe in themselves and to follow their hearts:

Believe in yourself and in your abilities. You have many talents and are supposed to work as a lightworker and healer and to be a steadying and nurturing influence for many.

Listen to the promptings of your heart. Do not doubt yourself and your journey. You know why you are here. You have chosen to come to be of service and this is the work you must do. You will always be provided for. Follow your inner guidance in all things, connect with Spirit and follow your intuition. You have pre-planned your life and it is on track at the present time.

I found out after our session that this young woman has written the Amazon bestselling book, *Pinch Me: How following the signals changed my life*, about the importance of following our gut feelings and signs from Spirit.

This advice was similar to this information given to a mother of young children who asked how she could reach her potential.

Continue to take time out for yourself and be open to the intuitive messages you receive. There will be signposts along the way and at the right time you will be drawn to the people that can help you. Just trust the process and believe in yourself.

A father of small children came to me because despite his best efforts he was not gaining any traction financially. With a family to support he was worried about this. I discovered that he had had many lives with an overtly spiritual focus, as a monk, priest and follower of a variety of religions. Consumed by work in this life he had neglected its spiritual aspects and his soul was crying out for attention. The information from his Akashic Record suggested that time spent concentrating on the needs of his soul and his spiritual development rather than obsessing about work and money would help him to reach his potential:

To progress on your path and to be more successful in all areas of your life more downtime is needed. In this new high vibration energy more is not better. Hard work gets results but time spent feeding the soul and doing what you love not what you feel you have to do will pay off. It is time to stop and take stock. Take time out just for you. Meditation at the same time every day on a regular basis will make a big difference.

You will make much more progress when you have connected

more with your soul self. You have experienced many lives and the happiest of these have been simple lives spent in nature. Ask yourself what will make you truly happy. Put the needs, restrictions and expectations of others aside and do what your heart tells you. Worrying about lack of money and scarcity restricts the flow and will create what you fear. Your soul is yearning for freedom and if you give yourself a little of that your businesses will start to prosper. As you connect more with your soul your true essence will emerge. When you live more authentically, your human fears and worries will stop closing in and enable you to step more fully into your true power and potential.

I found that in several other lifetimes this man had taken a Vow of Poverty. This was also preventing him from moving ahead financially. I was able to help him to relinquish this vow.

Irrevocably linked to the soul potential we bring into each lifetime is our life purpose and mission on Earth. This is chosen carefully before our birth to fit in with our innate talents, life situation, past life history and the greater good of humanity at the time. Our life purpose is often simple and doesn't come with a detailed step-by-step manual of how it will be achieved. There are numerous paths to God and many ways of reaching the same destination. There is flexibility in our life's plan to alter our course along the way. Some of us choose a more direct route, while others take frequent detours but eventually get back on track. The important thing is that we enjoy the journey.

The writer Dan Millman is a luminary in the life purpose area. In his groundbreaking book '*The Life You Were Born to Live*' he guides readers to work out their life purpose by using their birth date to determine a birth number of three or four digits which he then relates to their life purpose by utilising the positive and negative attributes of each number combination; this method is surprisingly accurate and informative. In his more recent work,

'The Four Purposes of Life: Finding meaning and direction in a changing world,' he says we essentially have four life purposes:

(1)   Learning life lessons.

(2)   Career and calling.

(3)   Our life path or hidden calling.

(4)   Attending to our purpose in each rising moment.

When asking about the life purpose of my clients I usually get information about their life lessons, career and the highest vision of their service to mankind during their lifetime. I love Millman's fourth purpose *'attending to our purpose in each rising moment'* because it infuses every second of our lives with expectancy, possibility and meaning.

The information I get on life purpose can be relatively straight forward, as in this reading for a friend who works in the natural health area, or more detailed:

> *Your purpose is to help anchor the light and to be a fount of peace and serenity for others to draw on for guidance and strength. You are already doing and being this for many and this work will grow in the future. At the moment you are a strong presence for those in your immediate sphere of influence but the plan is for you to work one-on-one with people to counsel, coach and heal them on many levels. In this work you will use words and your own innate and acquired wisdom plus some hands-on healing and energy work.*

This answer for a young currency trader named John contained more information:

> *Your soul purpose is to be a teacher. You have been a master teacher in other lifetimes. You are also a writer and*

there is potential for you to write books in the future. You would like to help others, men in particular, to go with the flow in life, to listen to and come from a heart space and to follow its directives. I see you working with individuals as a coach, teaching workshops and giving seminars to men who go against their natural rhythm and are pushing themselves to succeed and achieve (usually to fulfil the expectations of others). You can create a corporate package. You will teach your clients not to resist or try to force the order of things and to redefine their definition of success, which comes in all guises.

You will have a unique and down-to-earth way of relating which will appeal to these men and you will understand what they are going through. You will introduce a more heart-centred way of doing business and will teach your clients to connect with and follow their inner wisdom to help them be successful. You will encourage them to live in alignment with their values and inner truth and to learn that when they do this success will follow.

This all made sense to my client who despite huge effort and determination, was struggling to create financial freedom. He asked me whether he should abandon his work in the money markets.

Looking at your Akashic Record, being a currency trader is not your life's work but a stepping stone and a chance to prepare you for the more important work you will do in the future.

It could be counterproductive to just throw in this work and walk away. There are still lessons to be learned which will help you later on in your life to fulfil your soul purpose. Do some soul searching, get into your heart and look at why you are doing this and whether you really want to continue. If you stop putting so much pressure on yourself to succeed in this area and are less attached to how things will pan out (and any specific outcome) you could be in for a pleasant surprise. Sometimes we push ourselves too hard and this stops the flow. We are so bent on 'succeeding' that the energy we are putting out (which is often fear based) prevents what we are so desperately wanting to occur from happening.

Energetically, the desire for prosperity is out there so your chances of success are high but the timing must be right and everything in alignment. This is an important lesson for you to experience and learn and something, if you choose to follow the highest plan for your life, you can one day teach to others.

John is on track with his life purpose. This is what most clients want to know. A theme of this and many readings is the interrelationship between our life experiences and our life purpose. My work in the Akashic Records has confirmed for me that our life experiences perfectly prepare us for the work we have chosen to do. This preparation is often gruelling and throws up some challenges but is worth it. From personal experience I can say that there is no better feeling than living the life you planned and helping people in line with the vision you were born with.

Another client, Sandra, has a life purpose to help others to express their feelings and to deal with them in a healthy way. When I opened Sandra's Akashic Record I found that it was not just her childhood that had prepared her for her soul mission in this lifetime. She had been laying the groundwork over many lifetimes as well as in the period between lives:

You have a gift in this area. You have been challenged by and have gained mastery over your own feelings so are perfectly equipped to teach others. In your distant soul history you have been an addictive personality and have worked hard through many difficult lifetimes to overcome this.

In between lives you have been working with recently departed souls who have died as a direct result of drug and alcohol addictions. They have struggled in adjusting to 'life' in a 'body' that can't feed these addictions. You have run a sort of detox programme in Heaven and have worked with them to understand the reasons for their behaviour and the feelings they have been running away from. You have had great success with this programme on the other side. The plan has always been for you to do this work on Earth. The challenging times ahead will trigger fear and have the potential to make many of those with addictive behaviours worse.

If you choose to you will use many of the techniques you have learned in between lifetimes and will develop novel and unique ways of helping addicts. You will receive much help from your father and grandfather in spirit. They will bring you clients and do everything they can to help you be successful. This work will come naturally to you because you have done it before. It is your soul work.

In your biological family there is a history of addiction and by doing this work you will be clearing the energy imprints and tendencies in your family towards addictive behaviours. You have a soul connection with some family members from many lifetimes ago when you were as they are now and have offered to come and help to heal and clear addiction from your family line.

In reply to this reading I received the following email from Sandra:

"Thank you for my reading. And yes it fully resonated with me. In fact it brought tears to my eyes. There have been generations of addiction problems in my family. Sadly, I lost my father and grandfather to alcoholism."

Although there is a central theme to our chosen life purpose, our purpose is usually multi-faceted. This was the case with Sandra. She was:

> »   Teaching what she had once needed to learn.

> »   Carrying on the valuable work she had been engaged in, in between lives

> »   Fulfilling a soul promise and her contract with her extended family.

> »   And clearing and releasing the damaging vibration of addiction from her family line.

At this time of transition on Earth, we not only have the opportunity to re-write our contracts along the way but we can change our life purpose. The energy coming in as we upgrade from the Third to the Fifth Dimension is accelerating our soul growth and evolution and changing us so fast that the plan that we had before our lifetime may not fit any more. In Chapter 12, I tell the story of Clare. When I gave her a reading several years ago her life purpose was to help victims of injustice. When we met she had been trapped in a cycle of victimhood for many lifetimes. I worked with her to let go of this pattern and she has done this so dramatically and successfully that she says working with victims is no longer an option. She is studying to be a Real Estate agent which with its people and marketing orientation is not a job the 'old Clare' would have considered. In her words, "I am not a victim anymore so I cannot work with victims."

A reading I gave for an impressive woman called Kerry revealed a life purpose which is inextricably tied up with the future of her country, New Zealand, and its indigenous Maori people. Like Sandra she has been preparing for her current life for a long time. She has an ancient connection to this land and is here for a very important reason.

*You wanted to live here and you wanted the chance to make a contribution to the changing consciousness of New Zealand and of the world at this time. You have a close connection to this land having originally begun your Earth lives in the continent of Lemuria, of which New Zealand was a part. In this first lifetime you were a revered healer. You still carry these gifts and have the opportunity to use these again in this incarnation. You have had many lives in **Aotearoa** /New Zealand, firstly as one of the **Waitaha** race and thereafter as Maori.*

*You carry the mantle of a healer and **tohunga**. Those Maori with second sight have picked up on this. Your soul originated in the Pleiades which have a spiritual link with the Maori people who call them Matariki. The openhearted and loving nature of the Maori and their spiritual orientation comes from this Pleiadian connection. Your soul path has been from The Pleiades, to Lemuria and then to Aotearoa /New Zealand. It was felt you should be back at this time to help the people native to this land to walk into the light.*

You will have a way of working with and helping your clients that will resonate with them and many will be drawn to you. You will help heal the soul sickness, which has afflicted many Maori since European colonisation, by working on a deep physical, emotional and spiritual level. You will work with energy in a way that removes trauma, anger and fear and re-programme your clients so they can transform their lives. This work will seem miraculous to them and to their friends and families. You will be able to stop them harming themselves through self-destructive behaviours and to break cycles of unhealthy anger, addictions and violence.

You have always felt a close connection to this land and its indigenous people and want to help them at this important time in Earth's history to heal and release the past and to step back into their power. This is the lifetime you have been preparing for since your soul came to earth. This is the important one where you will draw on all the strengths and abilities you carry and have perfected during your many soul experiences.

Often our life purpose reflects our soul essence and personality. My friend, Ruth, has a life purpose that is inextricably connected with who she really is both on a soul and a human level. As a soul she originated from a far off star system and she has a soul history of courage, a thirst for adventure and great determination.

You originated in the star system of Epsilon Lyrae many years ago and were one of those who volunteered to come to Earth to anchor the codes of light. You were a being of love and great wisdom who was, and still is, adventurous and willing to accept and take on challenges. You have always been a highly motivated soul and one who has never been afraid to step out and put their hand up. You have had many testing lifetimes where you have suffered and been pushed beyond endurance but you have never given up.

I saw that Ruth's life purpose was to coach and inspire others to reach their goals and to display the strength of character, resilience and tenacity she has acquired during her many lifetimes. She has the ability to take coaching to a new level by guiding her clients to not only tap into and use their human talents and abilities but their soul gifts.

You won't just get people to recognise and reconnect with the talents and skills acquired in this lifetime but in all of their lifetimes. You will work with others to help them to understand, recognise and accept their innate abilities. You will be a soul coach not limiting yourself to the attributes of one life experience but helping your clients see the true magnificence and potential of their authentic selves. You will help these people to reconnect with the highest version of themselves.

The '**new children**' who have been incarnating in recent years have done so very consciously and often have a specific and clearly defined purpose for being here. Sam (who I mentioned in Chapter 6) whose mother, Belinda was worried about his increasing anxiety, has come back for the purpose of completion. His story resonated with me and my own understanding of my daughter Alice's life purpose. Once we move fully into the Fifth Dimensional energy it won't be as easy for souls who are carrying the emotional residue of difficult lifetimes on Earth to process and release it. I found that Sam was a soul who had only experienced Earth as a traumatic place and had been avoiding it for years preferring to incarnate in other places in the galaxy. If Sam wanted to complete his series of lifetimes on Earth and accelerate his soul progress he needed to be reborn at this time. It was now or never.

Sam has chosen to come to Earth now in an effort to complete his mission. He is terrified of being here but knows on a soul level that to evolve further he needs to come back and 'tie up loose ends.' He has avoided Earth for a long time preferring the vibration of other star systems where there is no fear, just pure love and acceptance. This is where he is from and this is the energy he carries. He has chosen to be incarnated at this time because the energy is so assisting of souls who want to deal with unfinished business and to balance their karma so they no longer need to return to this planet.

I also found that Sam came in with much to offer in his lifetime and that part of his life purpose is to be a teacher.

Being here at this time will also give him the opportunity to use many of his soul skills and abilities most of which have been learned in other galaxies. He has wisdom and talents which will help in Earth's transition and has the potential to be a much sought after teacher. His mission is to bring new knowledge and intergalactic wisdom to Earth. He is extremely special and has an important role to play.

Belinda has three remarkable children. They were born very close together. Gracie, the youngest was born only fourteen months after her brother Jack, who is two years younger than Sam. Belinda says she still doesn't know how it happened but it is obvious that Gracie, unlike her older brother Sam, was very eager to be here. Gracie was only several months old when I got this information through Belinda's Akashic Record:

Gracie is also a very special child. She is a Rainbow Child who has never been on Earth before. She is from a place of higher consciousness and total love and it is her mission to bring this to Earth and to help anchor the new energy. She does not need to be here but has chosen to be of assistance. She is a very wise and evolved being from another star system and has healing abilities and talents. She will adapt to Earth reasonably easily because she has been well prepared for this lifetime and mission. She has done her homework so to speak. She also is closely connected to Pleiadian energies and has a team of guides with her. She travels back to where she came from in her sleep state and will do this all her life.

These new children certainly hit the ground running! They are not weighed down by karma and negativity. Gracie as a newborn baby was already fulfilling her life purpose. I held her one day when I was feeling frazzled after teaching at the prison and felt waves of soothing energy surrounding me. Gracie has been carefully prepared for her mission and there is no doubt that she will help make the world a better place.

The potential for what we can create with our lives at this

momentous time on Earth is unlimited. The incoming energies are assisting us to release the beliefs and behaviours which have prevented us from realising our potential in the past. As we upgrade our thoughts we raise our vibration and anything and everything becomes possible. The higher purpose of our lives and of every moment of our lives is irretrievably linked to the process of global Ascension which is taking place. Watch this space! The time to recognise and realise our infinite potential is now!

Chapter 8
Family Ties

In between lives as we contemplate our next incarnation, careful thought is given to the human family we will be part of. The situation which will provide the greatest opportunity to learn our lessons and to fulfil our life purpose is usually chosen. Our choice of family often gives us the chance to continue relationships from other lifetimes, to address karma and to help souls we have a close connection with.

Parents, as key players, are carefully selected. They will help set the stage for the life to come. Both human and soul DNA aspects are taken into account and, with their life purpose in mind, the perfect balance is sought for each reincarnating soul.

Michael Newton in, *Destiny of Souls*, writes that it is common for souls to have several choices for each life and that in the life planning phase they are taken into a 'projection' room where they view the different options, evaluating the pros and cons of each. The incoming soul chooses their life situation after careful consideration. The determining factor is which option will best support them to fulfil their goals.

The environment a child is born into is central to this decision. From the moment of conception the development of a baby is affected by its surroundings—the physical environment of the womb and the emotional state of the mother. A growing baby is closely connected to its mother and is sensitive to her feelings. According to New Zealand's Brainwave Trust, at birth 15 percent of the brain is wired up and another 60 percent of the brain's neuronal pathways are laid down in the first three years of life. It is our experiences in these early years that shape the brain and provide the template for the life to come.

In infancy we take on core beliefs that many of us hold for life. If we end a lifetime in a traumatic way and then experience trauma at the beginning of the next, old beliefs and feelings we have had in previous lifetimes can be activated early on.

Most of us have no conscious memory of our past life or early childhood experiences but the core beliefs from our past are firmly embedded in our subconscious minds. If as Bruce Lipton says in his book, *The Honeymoon Effect* and Greg Braden in *The Spontaneous Healing of Belief* over 90 percent of our actions are governed by our subconscious minds then our early life experiences are crucial. In view of this it is not surprising that careful deliberation goes into planning our life circumstances and our choice of parents.

Each soul is different and while in many cases being born in a dysfunctional home and experiencing neglect and abuse may lead some to prison or worse, for others it can be a launching pad to success. The needs of each soul and their reaction to life events are entirely unique and their chosen situation is tailor-made to suit.

Careful thought is also given to the genetic DNA individuals will inherit and whether it will provide what each soul needs to fulfil its life purpose. Sometimes a child may have a short term contract with a biological parent because their genetic DNA is more suited to the larger plan for their life. That relationship may be short lived and they may have a separate contract with another soul to play the mother or father role.

My friend Lisa has four adult children. She asked why they had chosen her as their mother. The answers had one thing in common, they knew she would be a loving parent and would give them a good start in life. After that the reasons were very different.

Mike:

> *To help him to develop independence, resourcefulness and self-responsibility which are qualities that he carries innately but has not had the chance to hone in recent lifetimes. These qualities will be important to him in this lifetime and he has needed to strengthen these.*

Lisa has agreed to help her son, Mike reconnect with some important character traits and to help her other son, Nigel, to fulfil his life purpose.

Nigel:

> *To love him unconditionally and to show him other pathways and possibilities. To provide stability in his life and a safe haven for him to return to. To support him especially when he is helping himself but not to rescue or carry him. He is a special soul with a very close connection to you. You understand him and can see yourself in him.*

> *He is a highly evolved soul who has had lives of great influence as a healer and priest. He has more recently had a cycle of lives where he has chosen to experience suffering and challenges so he can become a master in dealing with and understanding human emotions.*

> *He has chosen you as his mother because of your strong soul connection and because he knows you can support him to find his life's work. This involves helping men who have experienced emotional intensity and disharmony to understand their feelings and to redirect this power in a positive way to help themselves and others.*

Lisa's daughter, Louisa, is giving her the opportunity to complete unfinished business and to address karma from a lifetime where they were separated.

Louisa:

To give her support and assistance with the difficulties she has chosen to experience in her family situation. To act as a sounding board and to give her the love and support you were unable to give her in a previous incarnation where you were her mother and forced to work away from your family. She loved you but was brought up by your mother, her grandmother who she felt was a poor substitute. It was difficult for you to live alone and away from your children and this is partly why you have chosen such a full-on family experience in this life.

Lisa as the mother of Emily is choosing to help a soul she has a close connection with.

Emily:

She chose you as a role model to show her what is possible. There is a close soul connection between you. She is like you in that she is balanced and wise, has healing, writing and speaking abilities and an important role to play in the New Earth if she chooses. She is already showing some of these gifts and there is a chance you could work together in the future. Emily has many similar attributes and abilities to you. She is destined to use them in a different way but to build on the work you do.

As is the case with Lisa and Emily, a child building on and expanding the work of their parent is a common theme in many of the readings I give.

There is almost always a karmic aspect to families. We choose to have in our family unit someone to whom we feel we owe a karmic debt or who owes us one. A soul feels the need to make amends to another soul or souls because of their past actions or inactions. There is a feeling of regret or distress because of behaviour which has resulted in the suffering of others and there is a desire to give back to that soul in some way to wipe the slate clean.

I don't believe that Karmic restitution is forced on us. It is our choice how, when and if we repay other souls for our past transgressions but I feel that the laws of the universe are such that there is a natural balancing out that occurs. I always told the teenage fathers I worked with in prison that what we put out comes back to us multiplied and to be careful what they did because it would boomerang back on them.

Karmic relationships are easy to pick. They are the difficult relationships, the people that trigger us, that evoke strong feelings and make us uncomfortable. It is difficult for us to look them in the eye and we often don't see 'eye-to-eye.' The saying goes, 'the eyes are the windows of the soul,' and when we look into the eyes of someone we have known before there is a glimmer of soul recognition. When we have hurt someone in an earlier lifetime and look at them intently it can be disconcerting and troubling—we are haunted by a past we can't consciously remember.

It is easy to fall back into old patterns and unhealthy behaviours that in the context of the present seem irrational and are difficult to understand. Most of us have a karmic connection with one or more of our family members. If there is a soul history of conflict and antagonism this can be entrenched and difficult to change. The family unit provides the perfect platform for addressing karma. The intimacy and intensity of family life throws up many opportunities for this as it is difficult to escape from these relationships.

A client, Alan, asked about significant past lives and found he had been a follower of Christ who was killed by the Romans. He has always had a difficult relationship with his mother and discovered that in this previous life she was the person who told the Romans where he was hiding.

Your last significant life on Earth was 2000 years ago at the time of Christ. You were one of his followers and were chased and murdered by the Romans following his crucifixion. There are those in your life now who stood against you and were responsible for your capture in that lifetime.

They have chosen to come back at this time as a way of repaying karma and to give themselves a chance to do things differently. Your mother still carries the guilt of what she did (or didn't do) in that lifetime and it is activated when she looks into your eyes. She did the best she could and was trying to protect her family and herself by revealing your hiding place. She loves you now and part of her soul contract with you is to address the karma from that time.

Another mother's past life karma with her adult son helped explain an intense outburst of anger that on the surface and in the context of her current lifetime seemed unfair. When she contacted me Marion had just spent a week with her son, Andrew, and her one year old grandson, Toby. During the visit Marion did all she could to help out but was still the target of her son's explosive temper. She was upset and disturbed after this visit and became ill. I helped her to see the higher version of what was happening and why:

I found that Andrew has chosen to deal with issues of anger and abandonment in his current lifetime. He has been dealing with these in a series of lifetimes, culminating in a recent one in France during World War II where Marion was again his mother. In this life Marion left him with relatives while she worked for the French Resistance. She was killed and never returned.

I found that Marion's grandson had come in to help his father. They are both starseeds from Andromeda—Andrew came thousands of years ago and Toby, more recently as a Rainbow Child, new to Earth. Toby's relationship with his father dated from Andromedan times and he was here to remind him of his true self and to bring up old memories and the issues Andrew had chosen to heal. I explained to Marion that there was truth in the angry words Andrew had spoken to her in the context of other lives but not this one, and that she was helping her son to let go of these feelings safely.

The episode had also helped her to release trapped emotions of her own. Their soul plan is for them to get closer in the future and for Marion to help her son rediscover and use the spiritual gifts he has been denying for many lifetimes. On a soul level, family relationships are always a two way street. They are 'win-win' with parent and child helping each other to evolve.

For those who have had challenging lives because the higher vibration energy they carry is threatening to those around them, help is now at hand. Reinforcements are arriving in ever increasing numbers with the modern day starseeds, the Indigo, Crystal and Rainbow Children, who carry a similar vibration. Many of my clients are grandparents who have a close relationship with grandchildren who are here to activate old memories and to reconnect them to their star heritage. Incoming souls always give careful thought to their family placements but none more so than these Star Children.

I met Jane, a mother of one of these children, at a dinner one night. Her son, Will is aged eight and is her only child. She shared with me her concerns for Will who sounded sensitive, talented and special. His mother had recently enrolled him at a new school because she felt his old one had not understood him or met his needs. He was different. They had tried, unsuccessfully, to make him fit a mould and were now trying to put a label on him. She was starting to doubt herself and her son and to wonder whether all the things her husband's family and some friends were saying about her over-protectiveness were right. She was losing heart and starting to think that she and Will might be the problem.

I tuned into her son through Jane's Akashic Record and found he was an enlightened soul experiencing his first life on Earth and finding the adjustment difficult. Although his first school had identified learning delays and difficulties, he was gifted with modern technology and computers in particular. Jane told me that he often made sage comments which stunned the adults around him. Within the Akashic Records I could see that Jane, a writer in her forties, sensitive, intuitive and dedicated to her child is the perfect mother for a son whose life purpose is to introduce to Earth new technology from more advanced parts of the galaxy. She is totally devoted, willing to go in to bat for him and is giving him the unconditional love and support he needs to flourish and to fulfil his mission.

Jane shared with me how easily she fell pregnant with Will. It was so quick and unexpected, she could hardly believe it had happened. She had just met his father and almost before they had a chance to get to know each other, he was on the way. She said she felt as if they were dealing with forces beyond their control—that he had selected his parents, brought them together and engineered things to give himself the best possible start in life.

Karen is the mother of two of these 'new' children, a daughter, Isabella, and Henry, a son who has been diagnosed as autistic. Henry's presence in her life precipitated the breakup of her marriage as her husband wasn't able to cope. Karen is now a single mother of two children, one of whom needs constant care and attention. She has given up her job as an accountant to look after her son and is now seeing some light at the end of the tunnel. Through Henry she has found her calling, working with autistic children.

She is also, through the gift of her child, learning her chosen life lessons which are:

> » *To learn to give unconditional love at the same time as providing strong boundaries and limits.*
>
> » *To remain true to and to believe in herself and her intuitive thoughts and feelings.*
>
> » *To learn patience and humility and the joy of giving to another without the expectation of anything in return.*
>
> » *To realise there are many things in life she has no control over.*
>
> » *To remain calm, centred and at peace no matter what is going on around her*
>
> » *To realise what huge strength and wisdom she possesses and to learn to love, value and accept herself.*

Henry is the perfect son for Karen. He has led her to her life's work. Karen is the perfect mother for Henry with her spiritual understanding, intuition and endless reserves of love, compassion and patience. Karen has a younger child, a daughter who is also playing her part in helping her mother find her soul work. With these two there is a soul connection which goes back in time, Karen being one of the original starseeds and her daughter, Isabella one of the new generation starseeds.

You chose (very bravely) to come to Earth as a starseed, embarking on a cycle of lives as a human being. You have experienced every aspect of being human from joy to suffering in many times, places and cultures.

The soul who is Isabella chose to stay in the stars but has come in now to remind you who you really are and to support you as you embrace your power and service work as a healer of the soul and psyche.

Isabella has her own work to do when she is older and it was important that she be born to a mother with a genetic makeup compatible with her soul DNA.

Isabella carries the codes of light that you and your mother carry and is a natural healer and leader.

Karen and Isabella are another example of a parent and child who may work together in the future.

There is potential for you and your daughter to one day help each other develop and refine your skills as healers and teachers.

Sometimes the best parent on a soul level is the one where the human relationship is far from easy. In answer to her question, "Why is there so much conflict and so many challenges in my relationship with my father?" one young woman got the following answer:

You have had lifetimes with your father where he has opposed and persecuted you. There has been a lack of trust between you in this life (because of these difficult past life experiences) and a strong sense of injustice and outrage at times. Sometimes your reaction to him has appeared extreme in the context of this lifetime but looking at the big picture over a number of lives it is understandable.

On a soul level you wanted the opportunity to make peace and to heal this relationship. He has helped you and is helping you to know and find yourself and your true identity and beliefs. He has acted as a catalyst to bring up qualities of strength of character, perseverance, leadership and openness which are a part of who you really are but which have lain dormant in recent lifetimes. The plan for this life is for you to reconnect with these aspects, to reintegrate them and to use them to be of service to others.

I worshipped my father as a child but our relationship was not always an easy one. He could be a hard taskmaster and he had a tendency to dwell on the negative. His criticisms probed my weakest and most vulnerable spots triggering all that needed to come up for healing and setting me on my life path. He died suddenly in 2013 which has left a gaping hole in our family. His legacy lives on, particularly in the way he valued the power of the mind and the importance of education. I can see now that he was the perfect father for me and I miss him very much.

Family composition is thoroughly considered by each incoming soul with the aim for each member being the successful completion of their respective missions. The synchronicities and symbiosis in families and the way members of all ages unconsciously work together to help each other evolve never ceases to amaze me. As souls we go to great lengths to set ourselves up for success in life. This is particularly the case for those, like my daughter Alice, who have a challenging path and a desire to break a chain of self-destruction in past lifetimes. She knew she would have to face the same challenges she hasn't managed to overcome previously but gave careful consideration to this life and what she would need to get through. She is surrounded by the love of a large and supportive family on both sides. She chose parents who she has a close soul connection with, are on a conscious spiritual path and would have the skills to cope. The other members of her immediate family were also carefully selected including our cat, Cobweb.

For the past fifteen years Cobweb has played an important role. She has been the angel we have needed and it is no accident that she came into our lives when she did. Cobweb has always had a special bond with Alice. From the day we brought her home she slept on Alice's bed and has been a devoted and loving companion. Her black and white fur started falling out in clumps when Alice became depressed and many times she let me know when Alice was in danger. She has comforted me through many sad and worrying days and for Alice has quite literally been a lifesaver.

Alice's brother, Hugh, who was her constant companion in his early years, is caring and responsible with an upbeat outlook on life. Hugh is a humanitarian whose life purpose (if he chooses) involves helping to relieve suffering in the developing world. Many of his previous lives have been cut short and he has died young. In this one he has not been able to grow up fast enough! He is independent and eager to make the most of his life.

From the moment Mary was born just before Alice's seventh birthday they have had a strong bond. Alice adores her younger sister and says she is a key reason she is alive and is starting to plan and envision a positive future. There is a close soul connection between these two. Mary is a highly evolved soul who does not have to be here for karmic reasons but has come in to help Alice and many others in the future. Her life purpose involves showing and teaching compassion and her early life circumstances and situation as Alice's sister are helping to prepare her for this.

Alice has helped us on many levels. She has propelled me into my life's work, brought my husband and I closer together, helped us face and overcome our worst fears, learn our life lessons and set her siblings on their path for the future. My husband, myself and two younger children are in our own ways the perfect parents and siblings for Alice. The situation is a gift. Alice is a gift. We are helping her to fulfil her life purpose and she is helping us with ours. In our family, as in all families, our life purposes and missions dovetail and overlap as we teach each other our chosen lessons and support each other to reach our potential. Again, all is perfect.

It is common for the same group of souls to incarnate together, being born over and over again in different groupings. To maximise our learning opportunities we swap and change roles. It is comforting to know that our closest relationships are eternal and that if we have regrets from one lifetime we will have the chance to make up for it at a later date. In my own situation I know that my husband and I have been together many times before and that I have shared lifetimes with my children. I wasn't surprised to find that my youngest daughter has also been my mother. I have often thought our roles should be reversed—she is much more sensible than me! I know I have lost Alice in a number of lifetimes and that one of the reasons I have agreed to be her mother is to repay karmic debt. I have a soul relationship with Alice that goes back a long way and wanted to help her in what I knew would be a supremely challenging lifetime. From a reading for myself:

> *You have a soul connection from many lifetimes and some karma but the main reasons you agreed to be her mother were:*

> » *To make up for your last lifetime when you felt unable to save people or treat them with respect and felt forced to go against the decent and humanitarian aspects of your nature.*

> » *Because there is a close bond on a soul level and you truly understand and love her. You wanted to help her and saw that this would give you the chance to learn your chosen lessons and to prepare you for your life's purpose.*

Lisa, mentioned earlier in the chapter, whose four children chose her for different reasons, has a busy family life this time round with her children, their father/her ex-husband, her current husband, sons-in-law and grandchildren as well as her '**family of origin**.' Lisa is playing a central role in the lives of all of them.

She struggled through childhood with learning difficulties and was bullied, overlooked and disrespected. She always felt different and not good enough. As I have found is often the case, on a soul level Lisa is highly evolved. An important part of her soul contract in this lifetime is to lead her birth family from the Third to the Fifth Dimension.

As I told her:

> *You were like the swan among a family of ducks who didn't fit in. You are no longer the ugly duckling and most of your family are starting to see this. Cast out as the weakest of the litter, your strength is now shining through for all to appreciate.*

In Lisa's case, the child who was overlooked and side-lined was following a sacred mission to help her extended family release some dark aspects so they could raise their consciousness and live comfortably in the higher vibration energy.

> *Your soul contract with your family of origin was to act as a trigger to bring their fears and negativity to the surface and then to provide a living example of unconditional love, forgiveness and of inner strength and fortitude. This is giving them the opportunity to connect with their divinity and to heal and release some dark energy that has been holding them back.*

> *You have been the light in the darkness and have contracted to lead your family into the New Earth. Some will choose to remain behind but many will follow you.*

Lisa's childhood was unhappy and difficult, she admits, but the future of her family is secure thanks to the sacrifices she has made on their behalf and her special grandchildren who are coming along behind her.

> *You have kept to your contract and have done your family a great service. Your granddaughters resonate with your energy*

and have come to give you support and assistance.

Lisa is a very happy woman who has touched the lives of many and has a soul mission in the future to inspire and delight many more. She has blossomed into a beautiful swan and no longer feels alone. My favourite saying, 'from tragic to magic' was borrowed from Lisa and it certainly sums up her life.

Most families at this time of transition have at least one member, like Lisa, who carries the light and is holding the space for the others to ascend. Having a higher vibration, these people often feel like they don't fit in or belong and are often mistreated and misunderstood. They have a contract with their families to perform this important act of service.

A client asking about her soul contract with her family received this reply:

> *In most families at this time there is a brave soul who volunteers to lead the way. They have the higher vibration, understanding and degree of soul evolution to act as a guide and support to those in their family who will not cope with the upheaval and changes ahead.*

I gave a reading to Tina who has shared many previous lives with her mother, father and sister. I found that she has a contract with them to help them move forward on both a human and a soul level:

> *You are the most highly evolved member of your family and you have agreed to help them to move forward with their own lives by moving forward in yours. You are to teach them the importance of love rather than fear, to help them shift into a new paradigm and to show them that growth can come just as easily from love as through suffering. Humanity has held the belief in their collective consciousness that suffering is necessary for soul advancement. This has been the case in the past but doing*

things the hard way is no longer necessary.

Tina's life purpose is to teach this important lesson to others. She works in a preschool with Rainbow Children who, holding the vibration of unconditional love, remind her on a daily basis of the power of love to transcend fear and human pain.

It is common for those with a special mission to have difficult circumstances early in life to provide the impetus they need to fulfil their life purpose. This is true for Tina who is honouring the soul contract she has with her family.

Your mother, father and sister have been with you in many lifetimes and have worked together to shut you down in some of these. They have asked for this opportunity to be with you again as a chance to do things differently.

There is so much you can teach them about love, humility and compassion and it is part of your soul contract to lead the way and to show them a different and higher way of doing and being.

I have met others who are providing a valuable service to their families. They have chosen a difficult path and have nobly and courageously agreed to clear and to purge their family of destructive tendencies and patterns which have been playing out for generations. Behaviour traits run in families and are part of our genetic DNA. Sometimes a positive legacy is passed down, sometimes it is the opposite.

One of my favourite jokes when I ran my parenting courses was, "What is the definition of a dysfunctional family?" The answer: "Any family with more than one person in it." always went down well.

Every family has its dysfunctional side. With the powerful influx of light over the past few decades the pressure has been on for families to heal and to bring their unhealthy aspects back into balance. In most families a brave soul has raised their hand to help with this and to 'take one for the team,' as the saying goes.

In her extended family both in the past and in the future, Alice is the lightning rod which is transmuting anxiety, fear and trauma for the rest of us. As she heals so does our entire family line. To release their families from unhealthy behaviours, souls may choose an intense experience—for example, alcohol or drug abuse. Through their own healing process they are able to liberate their wider family from the grip of addiction.

Tara came to me devastated by the losses she had experienced in her family. Death had never been far away, Cancer and suicide were the main causes. She was worried because the younger generation was in crisis with serious problems ranging from anger and violence to drug addiction and gang connections. The recent suicide of her nephew, Jack, had been too much to bear and she wanted to know what was going on.

Through the Akashic Records I found a complex family connection that went back to the Druids in England and involved two families of intertwined souls who have reincarnated together repeatedly. My client, Tara, had been a member of a pagan family that practiced sorcery and witchcraft. She was the one who carried the light. Her father didn't understand her or resonate with her energy but loved her deeply nonetheless.

In this past lifetime there was a nearby family of Druids who Tara gravitated to. She fell in love with one of them and, against her father's wishes, married him and joined their family. Her father didn't want to lose his daughter who he saw as a beacon of hope. Tara became ill and died and her father was heartbroken. He had lost her not once but twice and in his grief, he placed a curse on the Druid family which has resounded through time to the present day.

This curse had gained momentum through the centuries and had culminated in early and tragic deaths for many of the current family members as well as disturbing and destructive behaviours. This at-risk behaviour was at its worst among the younger generation of the family, several of whom had committed or attempted suicide, had psychological problems and serious drug addictions. Things often have to get worse before they get better and this was certainly the case with Tara's family.

Despite having trouble getting to our appointment (Tara said she felt like something was trying to stop her) once she arrived I received this information and realised it was time for the curse to be lifted.

I tuned into Tara's family and discovered they carried the vibration and the fear of death in their collective consciousness. So many family members had died they were all looking at each other and wondering who would be next. On top of the curse I discovered that a family history of depression and addiction had provided an opening for dark energy. This psychic attack was having a highly destructive impact on the family's younger members.

Working with Tara, I facilitated the lifting of the curse. Tuning into the soul of its perpetrator, Ivan, I found that he had made this oath without realising the possible consequences and repercussions. He had lost his beloved daughter and in his grief and ignorance had cursed the Druid family. He deeply regretted his actions and the way his angry words had hurt these souls throughout time. He had placed himself in limbo, a sort of 'soul no-man's-land' and holding place, until it could be lifted.

On the 12th of December, 2012, the timing was right. He had suffered from his actions almost as much as Tara's family.

On behalf of her family, Tara forgave him and liberated Ivan and their respective families from the curse and its effects. Ivan was freed from the past so his soul could continue to grow and evolve. Present throughout all this was Tara's nephew, Jack, who had taken his life not long before. He was still very much a part of the family and had not only arranged this long overdue healing but was keen to help its troubled younger members. Tara said she had felt Jack's presence very strongly in the two days before our session.

As well as a living member who leads the way, most families now have a loved one or loved ones in spirit who are working hard to help them during this significant time on Earth. Many souls, like Jack, have a soul contract which stretches beyond their physical lives whereby they agree to do all they can to assist and facilitate healing and completion for their families. It is helpful to have an angel in Heaven and most families have at least one member on the other side dedicated to guiding their families in this unprecedented time of change.

Unlike Tara I have lost very few family members in this lifetime. Since my father died, I feel him helping me often and so do my mother, four sisters and our children. He is still very much a part of our family and his loving presence is felt in many ways. With recent events in our large family he has been a busy man!

My nephew was married last year under a tree in a beautiful garden. Just as the vows were spoken a donkey in a nearby paddock started braying loudly and insistently. We were all sure it was dad letting us know he was there! Alice said she felt he was telling her to get on with her life. Knowing him, he probably was.

On a soul level, family ties connect us through time and space. We have a biological family and a soul family. If we are lucky we have someone in our lives who belongs to both. We reincarnate together repeatedly to address karma, support each other and to tie up loose ends from other lifetimes. Our family connections and interconnections are intricate and eternal.

These special relationships bring out the best in us ... and the worst. The intense environment of the family triggers deep emotions. Our families provide the backdrop of our lives and help us to learn to manage and master the strong feelings which are at the heart of the human experience. Whether we choose to belong to families who treat us with kindness or cruelty, the enduring power of the family is that it teaches us about love.

———————————————————————

Chapter 9
Love relationships

It is through relationships, in particular our love relationships, that we learn our most important lessons.

As a teacher of conscious parenting I taught that love, respect and trust were at the heart of a healthy relationship. I told parents that if their relationship with a child broke down it was because the child felt unloved, disrespected or that they couldn't respect and/or trust their parents. To improve a relationship they had to strengthen the mutual bonds of love, trust and respect. These connections are central to any successful relationship and closely linked to three of the most important lessons we come to Earth to learn.

How to:

» Give and receive love.

» Respect others and to command respect for ourselves.

» Learn to trust others, be someone who can be trusted and to trust ourselves.

Our learning about love extends to unconditional love, love of self, compassion and the ability to forgive. In learning respect we learn how to treat ourselves and others in loving ways and how to put boundaries in place to protect us from the harmful behaviour of others. Learning to trust and be trustworthy involves taking total responsibility for our choices and behaviour. Manipulation, emotional and physical abuse, co-dependence and other controlling behaviours all come from fear. Love, trust and respect carry the love vibration.

At this time on Earth we are moving from fear to love. Our relationships, and in particular our intimate ones, are giving us the chance to do this. They are helping us find our true selves, to speak our truth and to learn how to work in partnership. They are a fast track to mastery.

As a child I dreamed of growing up, falling in love and living happily-ever-after. As a young woman I thought the hard part would be finding the right man to marry. Looking back on a 36 year relationship with my husband, Marty, I realise I was wrong. The hard part comes after the wedding. I love my husband deeply. We have shared many lives before this one and it feels like several lives within this one. As the years pass I am full of gratitude for the stability this relationship has given me and for this opportunity to learn and grow together at such an important time on Earth.

Marty and I are very different people from the twenty-year olds who met as students in 1978. In our wedding photo, we look young, fresh and innocent. We had no idea what was in store for us, of the respective healing journeys we would face in our thirties and forties with their many twists and turns ... or that just as we had both faced our demons and reached a place of inner peace and joy, this would be threatened by a 'lurking enemy', we had not seen coming, our daughter's mental illness. Our life together has sometimes been a roller coaster, a ride not for the faint-hearted, but like the best wine our relationship has matured and improved with age. It has been a vehicle for the learning of our life lessons and the balancing of karma. It has been an opportunity for two souls who have been connected throughout time to work in partnership and to learn healthy behaviours.

While we have our differences, we also have much in common. We have not been afraid to do the inner work on ourselves and the outer work on our relationship. We are both thinkers and writers who like to go beneath the surface and explore. We have followed our hearts in searching for our life purpose and we both embarked on a conscious spiritual path in our late thirties. We have come at it from opposing angles but in the middle there is a solid platform of common ground. We are both proud, loving and committed parents. There has been important learning in this relationship which has spanned nearly two-thirds of my life and which will hopefully last for years to come.

The relationship teachings of Harville Hendrix resonate with us both. The basis of his 'Imago Theory' is that it is a subconscious desire to heal our childhood wounds that attracts us to our mates. He says that in order to heal and become whole we unconsciously select partners who are similar to a parent we had a difficult relationship with as a child and/or have the characteristics we have disowned as children.

In my *Heart to Heart Parenting* courses, I described how despite a parent's best efforts we can get shut down as children and take on core beliefs that we carry through life. To teach this I told this story:

One day I was waiting in a long queue at the counter of a 'Spotlight' haberdashery store. In front of me was a young mother with her own mother, a baby in a stroller and a small child of about twenty months of age. They had a pile of fabric and had obviously been there a while. Suddenly the toddler left her mother's side, running through the shop shrieking and laughing as she weaved in and out between customers and bolts of fabric. Her grandmother walked over to her and demanded she return to the line.

"Get back over here now!" The little girl did as she was told for about five seconds and then took off again, noisily careening through the shop. This time her grandmother was furious. She stalked over to her granddaughter, took her arm and dragged her back. She spoke loudly and angrily.

"Behave yourself! Stop being naughty! You were going to stay with me tonight. You were going to stay with grandma tonight but you can't now because you're not good enough."

I was horrified. This is how it happens, I thought. Very early on in life we get told we are not good enough. We internalise the messages we receive as children especially from adults who we think know everything. After these experiences we change our behaviour, adopting a 'false self'—an inauthentic persona designed to gain the approval and love of our caregivers which we feel is vital to our survival. As a result of an experience like this, this little girl might decide that it is not safe to be adventurous, independent or joyful and shut down or disown these qualities. It is these attributes so 'imago theory' goes, that in an effort to heal her childhood wounds, this child will one day look for in a partner. She may also look for someone who is angry and vulnerable to shame in order to heal her childhood relationship with her grandmother and she may take on the belief, 'I am not good enough.'

These theories made sense to Marty and me. We went to a weekend Imago course in Auckland which at the time I found threatening. We were asked to be honest with each other on a variety of issues. Marty told me he didn't like my 'uncared for' feet. The weekend touched some sensitive spots and by the time we drove home over the Bombay Hills we were yelling at each other. Despite this we liked these ideas and could see how our relationship was giving us the opportunity to address and heal our childhood issues.

I have always been sensitive to criticism and with the energy of shame, self-hatred and victimhood I brought into this lifetime, as a child suffered from my father's tendency to notice life's imperfections. This characteristic of his was at its worst during my childhood when, as the father of five children and a manager responsible for many employees, he was sometimes stressed and under pressure. Marty also grew up in a large family. He had two older and two younger siblings and a hard working, war veteran father who was not often emotionally available. He would have liked more of his father's time and attention.

When we had been married for several years, had started a family and Marty was working in a job he disliked as a partner in a large law firm, the pressure came on. Unhappy in his work, my husband started to notice my shortcomings. Like my father before him, he was critical of me and the way I did things. My reaction to this was to focus my attention onto my children and everyone else. I distanced myself, keeping him at arm's length just as he felt his father had done. This was painful until we were able to see and understand the bigger picture. A classic Imago couple, we triggered each other's issues from the past, bringing our childhood pain to the surface for healing.

When I married my idea of a perfect relationship was straight out of a fairy tale. Love would reign supreme and there would be no friction or discord. This is a worthy goal from a human perspective but during the 29 years since I have found the soul's definition of a perfect relationship to be very different.

The human part of us which yearns for 'happily ever after' peace and contentment is at odds with our soul selves which view love relationships as our greatest opportunity for learning and as catalysts for healing and growth. This has been my experience and the experience of many I work with.

The Akashic Records enable us to take Harville Hendrix's Imago Theory one step further (or back) beyond the childhood of our current lifetime to all of our lifetimes and to all the relationships we have had throughout time. At this momentous time on Earth we are healing from the effects of many lifetimes, not just this one.

Our soul is focused on resolving these past experiences and will present us with opportunities for this. As discussed earlier, careful consideration is given in the pre-life planning phase to creating the perfect conditions for this to happen. My work in the Records indicates that our main lessons are learned through relationships. Given this, who we spend our life (or any part of our life) with is crucial.

As the world raises its vibration, completion in all areas is the order of the day. Souls with unfinished business with others and karmic debt are keen to have the opportunity to balance the scales so they can step with a sure footing into the energy of the New Earth. Soul contracts to redress karma are one of the reasons why some of us have multiple relationships and also why in recent years many relationships have ended without the heartbreak and acrimony of the past. When karma has been repaid and our contractual obligations have been met we know it on a soul level and it is easier to move on.

In the new energy, people can change, relationships can change, karma can be erased and contracts re-written. Anything is possible. Sometimes it is easier in the long run to stay with the same partner to learn our lessons. As the saying goes you can leave a relationship but the dirty washing will still be in your suitcase and will eventually have to be sorted. Having said this, if the vibrational difference between a couple becomes too great it is often impossible to bridge the gap. In this case both partners may be better off unpacking and dealing with their baggage by themselves!

In the Records I have found much evidence to support the theory that we attract or choose the perfect partner to heal our childhood wounds. From a soul point of view a perfect relationship is one where we act as triggers to bring up pain from our childhoods and past lives for healing.

This was definitely the purpose of my relationship with Marty in its early days. One of our cars was a tiny Suzuki Alto which I often used to transport our children. Around the corner from our house was a typical Wellington street, on a slope with speed bumps at regular intervals. The high point of my children's day was whizzing down that road in our tiny car. "Bumpy road, bumpy road !" they would cry and I would take a detour so we could travel down that road and feel the thrill of the bumps. My relationship at this time was like this road as Marty and I excavated each other's buried pain. Navigating this with three young children and all the pressures that go with this took some doing. Luckily we were both willing to work on our relationship and to dig below the surface to try to gain a deeper understanding of what was going on.

Sophie, like many of my clients, asked about her relationship with her boyfriend, Dave. He loved her but was not willing to make a serious commitment. In her late twenties she had seen many friends marry and start families and wanted the same for herself. Her rising anxiety as her biological clock started to tick was pushing her dream of marriage and children even further away. Going into her Record there was a familiar pattern:

This relationship is acting as a catalyst to bring issues you carry to the surface for healing. This is the purpose of many relationships and is one of the purposes of yours and Dave's.

It was also clear that within this relationship were many of the lessons Sophie had chosen to learn:

Your learning in this relationship is that you cannot control the outcome of a situation and how a person behaves and that sometimes the most loving thing you can do is let them go. You have chosen to learn lessons about control and allowing others freedom and independence. This relationship is also supposed to teach you about enjoying the moment and not thinking too far ahead or pre-empting anything. There is genuine love in this relationship but Dave is an adventurous soul and has never been easy to pin down. He marches to the beat of his own drum and your learning is to respect this and to see and understand what he needs to do for his highest good.

As is often the case in relationships there was a karmic element:

You had a life long ago where you were the male and Dave was your wife and he was the one you left behind when you went on your adventures. You were away for years at 'The Crusades' and Dave (your wife) was left to take responsibility for your children. This karmic imbalance is being redressed in this lifetime.

Most of my clients have relationship questions. Many come to me hoping for good news about an unhealthy relationship. It is a huge responsibility passing on such information and an aspect of my job I find difficult. I don't want to break any hearts but it is patently obvious when a relationship is not in a couple's best interests. It is certainly not my place to tell someone to end a relationship. I help them see the bigger picture and what the learning is for them and leave them to decide what to do. We have contracts with all those we have relationships with. Some of these are short term with a specific objective (for example, to provide the right genetic mix for a child) and others are lifelong. Most relationships serve as a catalyst for healing as well as providing the opportunity to learn lessons and to address karma and unfinished business from other lifetimes.

Nina is a single mother who is trying to move beyond a pattern of unhealthy relationships with men. Her relationships have been the triggers for soul healing and growth.

You have had a series of recent lifetimes where you have been female and have been controlled and dominated by those around you (usually males). In most of these lives it has been difficult for you because you lived in societies and cultures where women were second class citizens and dependent on their husbands.

In this lifetime Nina is determined to let go of this pattern:

> *You are on an accelerated path and have chosen to clear*
> *the decks, so to speak, and to change behaviours that have kept*
> *you stuck for many lifetimes.*

To set the stage for this Nina chose to have a complex relationship with her father as a child and several unhealthy relationships with men as a young woman. These men have helped her learn her lessons. As I found in her Record :

> *It is not your responsibility to make any man happy. It is*
> *important to realise that when your father was unhappy you*
> *were not to blame. He was doing the best he could at the time*
> *but you are closely connected and you felt it was your fault*
> *when he was troubled and angry. This is a big learning for you:*
> *to detach yourself from the energies, actions and feelings of*
> *those around you and not to feel you are to blame for how they*
> *are choosing to live their lives or that it is your job to fix things.*
>
> *This tendency to 'rescue' has resulted in you being treated*
> *badly by male partners in this life and in others. You have*
> *given openly, lovingly and generously of yourself and it has not*
> *been appreciated. This relationship has also taught you about*
> *unconditional love with boundaries. It is possible to love and*
> *accept someone exactly as they are but to put up boundaries to*
> *protect yourself from actions and behaviours that are damaging*
> *to you.*

Her experience with her father was a perfect starting point for her chosen lessons in this lifetime. The series of unhealthy relationships she has had as a young woman have mirrored her relationship with her father.

> *These relationships have also helped bring up emotions*

and sadness from your childhood and some of the issues you have with your father in this life and this also was part of their purpose.

Karma has been at the heart of many of Nina's relationships and she has also chosen in this lifetime to attend to unfinished business.

There has been unfinished business from other lifetimes between you and these partners. One reason you have chosen to reconnect with these men is so you have the opportunity to balance karma. The karma has been mainly on their sides and they have not all taken advantage of the opportunity to treat you differently and better than in the past.

This time round Nina has chosen to learn discernment. Feeling a strong attraction to someone does not necessarily mean they are right for us. It is common to feel a strong connection with souls we have known before. This magnetic pull can mean we end up in relationships that are not only unhealthy in this life but have been in others. These relationships may be challenging on a human level but are exactly what we need if we are to evolve as souls.

When we meet people who we have had other lifetimes with even if the experiences have not been good we feel the connection to that person and this strong energy can sometimes be mistaken for love.

The relationships we have with those around us also reflect the relationship we have with ourselves. The first step to finding a healthy love relationship is learning to love, trust and respect ourselves. This is what the Akashic Records suggested was in Nina's best interests:

At this stage in your life your most important relationship is with yourself. You are on a journey of self-discovery which will lead to self-love and acceptance. It is important to make your relationship with yourself a top priority.

These relationships have enabled Nina to do some deep soul healing and to overcome a debilitating pattern of many lifetimes.

You are a soul who has given too much of herself and has often been taken advantage of. This pattern has been repeating over many lifetimes and you decided to re-experience it in this lifetime while you are young so you can get a good taste of what you no longer want.

Relationships are mirrors that reflect back our unhealthy aspects. We can clearly see these ... if we are willing to look. When I ran my parenting courses I talked about healthy relationships and advised parents not to use the 'b' or the 'f' word ... which were ... of course ... 'blame' and 'fault.' Projection is where we transfer the feelings and behaviours we are not willing to own in ourselves onto others. What we think is all about the other person is really all about us. Relationships help us to learn to take responsibility for our behaviour.

Present day relationship difficulties can also have their roots in previous lives. Joe, in his mid twenties, was having problems creating a lasting relationship. In his Akashic Record I saw that the anxiety he felt about relationships and getting close to people stemmed from tragic events in his most recent past life.

His three children had died in the Aberfan Mining disaster in Wales in 1966. A landslide from a mine fell onto the village school, killing 144 people, mostly children. Several months after this, he also lost his wife when unable to cope with her loss, she committed suicide. He took on some beliefs in this lifetime which continued to affect him.

You were heartbroken and never recovered from the loss of your family. You were grief stricken and depressed and didn't live for long afterwards. You died carrying the belief that you always lose those you love.

I could see that this pattern of losing loved ones had been present in other lifetimes. Another recurring theme of betrayal by those close to him was also making it difficult for Joe to find a partner:

You carry the belief, 'It is not safe to love,' and a feeling of mistrust which comes from being betrayed by lovers in other lifetimes. This pushes those you would like to get close to away. You are sending out mixed messages and that is why it has been difficult for you to create a happy and lasting relationship.

His subconscious was trying to protect him from the pain he remembered on a cellular level.

You are unconsciously trying to protect yourself from being hurt again by building a wall around you. This has not made it easy for you to get close to people.

I was not at all surprised when I found that Joe's life purpose was inextricably linked to his relationship challenges.

This lifetime is all about recognising and overcoming these patterns and tendencies. Your life purpose is to fully open your heart again and to help others to do the same.

In another case, I answered the phone to find a distraught man on the line. A year before his wife had been struck by a vehicle and killed while out walking. It had taken a while for her body to be found and when it was it was obvious her death was intentional. The man who killed her was about to be tried for murder and this man, James, was beside himself. He couldn't understand why he had lost his wife so tragically and came to me for a reading.

Like most couples James and his wife, Amie, have a soul connection and have been together before. In this lifetime, Amie, had agreed to die young to help James with his soul growth and to provide an opportunity for him to rediscover and use the unique gifts he has ignored for many lifetimes. I told James:

> *This was planned. On a soul level you felt you needed something dramatic to happen so you could wake up to your true self. You have many spiritual gifts and talents which have not been used in recent lifetimes. You have veered off your path and this lifetime is about pulling yourself back on track. Amie is a soul who has known you through many incarnations and cares about you deeply. She wanted you to have the opportunity for huge growth and agreed to play her part. You have had a series of lifetimes of blocking out your spiritual nature and have felt deep regret for your untapped potential.*
>
> *Amie offered to lose her life in this tragic way to precipitate the change in you. You have special abilities and the plan is that you will use them in this lifetime to help others. You did not want to give yourself the chance to turn your back on your talents this time round and that is why you chose such a devastating experience.*
>
> *You have been a healer, a shaman (holy person who heals and passes on spiritual information) and a skilled public speaker. You have these strengths still and the plan is for you to use them to lead and inspire others. If Amie had remained in her body your spiritual talents and abilities would not have had a chance to come forth. You would have remained in her shadow and it would have been too easy for you to follow the same road as in recent lives where you have suppressed and shut out your spiritual side.*

Even though his wife was dead, it was reassuring for James to know that Amie's soul contract with him had not ended and she was still with him.

It is important for you to realise that she is not gone. She is still just a thought away. From where she is she has an expanded view of everything. She can see your soul's path and your soul history. Her contract with you is to help you to reach your potential in this lifetime. She can more easily and effectively help you out of her body. She understands the difficulties you have faced and loves you unconditionally and will always be with you helping you to move forward and to reclaim your spiritual birthright.

Her contract with you involves helping to bring you home to your true soul nature. She was doing that in the months leading up to her death by trying to get you to realise some eternal truths. She was setting you on course for what was to come. She was activating the memories of the part of you that you have ignored for many lifetimes. She was making you think and preparing you to cope with the far-reaching impact of her sudden death. Her contract with you is not over and she will be working with you actively to help you on your path and to guide you on your way.

There was further guidance and reassurance for James in the Records.

At the moment it is important to take one day at a time. You have much love around you and the people that can help you at each stage of your journey will appear as if by magic. You are receiving much help from Spirit at this time and you don't need to do anything except look after yourself so you can cope with the trial and the anniversaries coming up. There has already been much learning for you in this situation and this will not stop. Despite the circumstances of Amie's death you will come, through the love and actions of others, to see and understand human nature at its best and this will transform you.

In a few years you will be a completely different person. Your soul self will start to emerge and with it your ancient gifts. This will happen slowly. In the future you have the potential to be a sought after public speaker and a healer, working specifically with those dealing with shock and overwhelming emotions. You are a gifted writer and you will be able to pass on your soul wisdom and the lessons you are learning in a way that ordinary people will be able to relate to and understand.

The soul contract between this couple did not end with Amie's death. They are still working together for their highest good and to assist in each other's growth.

Soul relationships transcend time and space to help us to know and understand our true selves. Human relationships are mirrors placed in front of us. They reflect back the impact of our behaviour, forcing us to face up to the truth of who we are. It is difficult to hide from ourselves in a relationship and the best ones are those that help us to grow and develop in all areas of our lives. Through our relationships we connect with the same souls in lifetime after lifetime in many different roles. Our relationships take up where they left off in each incarnation and it is easy to step back into old habits which are counter-productive. The challenge is to leave these behind and to focus on the privilege of sharing life with a soul mate whose path has been linked with ours for centuries.

I am realising the gift of my relationship with my husband, which has spanned nearly four decades in this lifetime and thousands of years on a soul level. I am grateful for the opportunity to share my life with such a noble soul. We have had our moments as we have challenged each other and reflected back the human foibles we have picked up along the way but with Marty's help I have learned some of my most important lessons. After some challenging years we have both, individually, come to a place of self-love and acceptance which has given us a solid foundation for greater intimacy and a true soul partnership.

The history we have with our soul mates is precious. We may have made mistakes with them in the past but that doesn't mean we have to make them now. There is the potential with each of these soul friends of ours to create a lasting and fulfilling relationship. This is our birthright and no less than we deserve.

Chapter 10
Past Life Trauma

All three of my children have shown signs of past life trauma. I believe that on a soul level, Alice has been releasing memories of her traumatic experiences on Earth. She has carried these memories and their energetic imprints for lifetimes and has come back now when the energies are so assisting of this process to honour her soul's desire for healing.

My work in the Records has confirmed my belief that every cell of our body is like a mini Akashic Record and that in our cellular DNA we carry the memories of all of our human experiences. Our cellular memory stores in the physical what the Akashic Records hold in the etheric.

Cellular memory is the memory of past events, feelings and trauma that is held within the DNA in every cell of our body. There are many documented cases of 'inherited cellular memory' where organ recipients have noticed changes after transplants. New food preferences are the most common but others have noted changes in mood, values, music and tastes and in other personal characteristics. Here I am talking about cellular memory on a soul level—the idea that our cells not only hold memories from our current lifetime, but from all our lifetimes and soul experiences. I believe that the DNA of each cell carries not only our genetic blueprint but our soul blueprint and that soul memory in partnership with our genetic DNA lays down the template for both our human and soul potential.

Kryon, channelled by Lee Carroll in his book *The Twelve Layers of DNA*, talks about the different energetic layers within the DNA of our cells. He says these are quantum layers and that the eighth layer holds our Akashic Record and that the ninth is a healing layer worked with by St Germain. As well as in our cellular DNA, Kryon says that in the auric field around our body there exists an energetic record of our soul's journey.

When I started giving readings I just passed on information. Then I was guided to use the high vibration of the Records for healing. I was directed to work with St Germain and his violet flame to clear clients' physical and energy bodies of limiting beliefs and behaviours. I wasn't quite sure why and how it worked but it did and the Kryon channellings have given me wonderful confirmation.

The memories of our previous lifetimes are held within the DNA of our cells and in our energy fields. Once triggered, these unconscious memories manifest through physical, mental or emotional pain. As well as trauma and limiting beliefs from past lives we also carry the memories of our gifts, talents and soul potential. These memories can be activated simply by being back in a human body. This is particularly true for souls who have had few lifetimes on Earth and are used to living in the higher dimensions. Memories can also be triggered when we feel the same emotions or have similar experiences to those from an earlier incarnation or when we reach, in our current lifetime, the age we were when previous trauma occurred. Past life trauma and memories can also be evoked by sensory experiences such as a smell, taste, music, art or a place. We can be reminded of the past (and sometimes the distant past) through a déjà vu type of experience. I have worked with many whose return to a human body has brought up feelings of limitation and has triggered what seem like irrational fears.

Samuel, a young man in his early thirties, came to me asking for clarity. He told me that as a child he was shy with low self-esteem.

This got worse at the age of twenty. "I became socially isolated," he told me. I discovered that Samuel had lived few Earth lives, most of which had been challenging, and that being back in a human body had brought up negative memories and fears that his soul wanted to release:

As a child you were shy and suffered from low self-esteem as past life memories of the density and difficulty of your previous Earth experiences returned. You have never felt comfortable in your body and knew on some level that choosing a human life had disempowered you. You have been experiencing life in other star systems where the higher vibration is a better match to yours and the energies are lighter and more loving than those on Earth.

On a soul level you knew you had to return at some point to face the emotional challenges of being human and deal with some of the dross that has accumulated during some difficult life experiences. You made this choice because it is necessary if you wish to evolve further.

I found that he had chosen to return to a physical body now because as Earth moves to a higher frequency its energies would help him with this process:

You have come back now because you have unfinished business. You want to use the energies we are moving into to clear karma and transmute and release negative thought patterns and beliefs your cellular memory has been carrying from past lives on Earth.

Samuel's Akashic Record also revealed that in his most recent past life he had been attacked and killed by people he knew and trusted. These memories were stored in his cells and were a trigger for the social phobia he experienced at the age of 20 in his present lifetime.

Your feelings of social isolation became stronger at 20 because at this age in your most recent Earth life some people you were trying to help, turned on you and you ended up being burnt at the stake. As you died you carried the belief that getting close to people and trying to help them is dangerous and that it is safer to be alone. This memory was reactivated at the same age in this life when this past life trauma occurred because your cells still carry this belief.

Since he was a child, Samuel has had a habit of compulsively twisting and pulling his hair during his sleep. He asked about these 'night terrors' and the answer I received showed the depth of his past life trauma:

This is a flashback to your last human life. You were someone who was always different from the others in your village. You were kind and had healing abilities so when people were unwell they started coming to you. You gave your time freely and with an open heart and had great success in healing the sick. An epidemic came to the village and was so virulent that you were powerless to stop it and many died. The villagers were superstitious and in their grief wanted someone to blame. You hadn't been able to help them on this occasion and they focused on your differences and some of your practices which they decided involved the use of witchcraft.

From being the person they turned to for help and comfort, you became the villain. The leader of the village who had lost most of his family decided you had cast a spell over the community. You weren't killed immediately because you had some supporters and it was a controversial move.

You spent several months in a prison cell with very little food and clothing and you started to lose your mind. During this time you got into the habit of twisting and pulling your hair.

The memories of this lifetime are still fresh and return when your body is relaxed and in a sleep state. They are ready to be released.

I have had many clients with physical illnesses that are related to injuries from other lifetimes. I guided a friend who was suffering from back pain through a past life regression. She saw herself in a medieval battle, being trampled on by a horse. Her back was broken and she died. As many regressionists have found the triggering of soul memory has a healing effect and my friend's pain quickly disappeared.

This type of healing on a cellular level is central to the work of Brian Weiss. In the 1970s, Weiss was a traditional psychotherapist who used hypnotherapy to help his patients uncover repressed memories. One day he asked his patient, Catherine, to go back to the source of her current problems and she was transported back to another lifetime. In subsequent sessions she returned to other incarnations and the period in between lives which the Tibetans call the 'bardo' state. Brian first wrote about these experiences in his book *Many Lives, Many Masters*, and he has been a leader in the field of regression therapy ever since.

A friend had a recurring rash on her forearms for several years. She had visited many skin specialists and homeopaths and had unsuccessfully tried everything from a change of diet to expensive creams. When I accessed her Record I discovered that a difficult work situation had activated memories of strong emotions she'd felt when she burnt to death in another incarnation:

Your skin rash was triggered by a stressful incident at work that revived the cellular memory of when you were burned in a previous life. Your current feelings are the same as the feelings you had then—helplessness, desperation and of being trapped and powerless.

When the rash appeared you were the same age you were when you died in the fire in this past life. You were trapped in a burning building and unable to escape. The rash has appeared on the part of your arm that you held up to protect yourself from the flames. You felt the pain when your arm was burned, then lapsed into unconsciousness from smoke inhalation and died. The cells in your arm still hold the memories of that event.

Recently my friend Jill lost her father shortly after she had an operation for carpal tunnel syndrome. During surgery the surgeon made an incision in the palm of each hand. Jill took time off work to recuperate and her hands were healing well until her father's sudden death. Almost immediately her scars flared up and the pain was, she said, much worse than before the operation. As the weeks passed, the pain remained. A single parent for over 20 years Jill had been very close to her father, talking to him most days. She was overwhelmed by grief which, because of her demanding job, she had little chance to express. I offered to access her Akashic Record and discovered that the pain was directly linked to her sadness and that over many lifetimes, including one in the time of Christ, her hands had become a symbol of suffering.

The aching in your hands is connected to your grief. You are in so much emotional pain that it needs an outlet and that outlet is your hands. Once you come to terms with your loss the pain will lessen. The hands also represent suffering to you. You have a soul history of speaking out against injustice and have often been persecuted for this. You were one of those who lived at the time of Christ and watched his crucifixion. You feel as if your heart has been crucified. This is another reason why there is so much pain in your hands.

I found further evidence of this theme in Jill's Akashic Record. I saw her suffering in various lifetimes with her hands tied above her head as she was flogged and behind her back as she was whipped and as she was burnt at the stake. I saw her being tortured on a rack with her hand and arms out-stretched and having a hand cut off in an Islamic lifetime. Jill's immediate past life was as a prisoner of war and I found her hands featured in this lifetime as well:

I see you with your hands tied up when you were captured and force marched to the prison camp and also when you were punished inside that camp. You have not had time to process and deal with the emotional pain you have been feeling and it has had to come through your hands.

As an afterthought I also got the following:

You carry the belief that your 'hands are tied' in your job. You feel stuck in your current situation, and don't have the freedom you would like.

This made sense to Jill who, after years of being self-employed, has taken on a prestigious but demanding government job. She managed to get time off work and with some help has been able to let go of her grief. Her hands have now healed and she is pain free.

Many of us carry physical weaknesses from other lifetimes. In my case my respiratory system is affected. I enjoyed good health until Alice became ill and then I developed asthma and sinus problems. My health issues were undoubtedly triggered by stress but also, I am certain, by re-experiencing the same emotions I have felt as I have died in many lifetimes, struggling for breath. Alice's illness was such a shock and she was so unwell that I often literally held my breath over the next few years. Through accessing my Akashic Record I discovered that I have suffered from chest and lung ailments in many lives—from a Mayan lifetime, where I was buried alive in a pit to those where I died in fires or suffered from lung diseases. In a lifetime in Europe in the mid-19th century, which has parallels to this one, I came down with consumption (tuberculosis) at the age of 46 (when I developed asthma in my current life) and I died of this illness aged 54.

A sudden and traumatic death traps a vibration of fear and intense emotion in our cells. A life that ends suddenly and unexpectedly also carries with it a feeling of incompleteness, of unfinished business that needs to be resolved. Author Carol Bowman has written about the past life memories of children and she says it is common for them to remember experiences from previous lifetimes. She believes that these memories are usually strongest between the ages of two and five and that they often relate to traumatic deaths in past lives. She says the soul has a desire to heal and that these memories easily surface in young children and can explain nightmares, phobias, night terrors and unusual statements or behaviour. A young child may suddenly talk about something that has happened and things they can't possibly know in words that are advanced for their years. They may talk about "When I died before" or "When I had my other mummy," and go into an altered state where they speak wisely and matter-of-factly. Parents know there is something special and other worldly happening. It is as if time is suspended and their child's soul is speaking to them. They get goose bumps or a surge of energy running up and down their spine The magic moment ends as quickly as it began and their little boy or girl goes back to being a child again.

Carol Bowman describes how her son, Chase, had a spontaneous past life recall when he was five. Listening to the noise of fireworks on the fourth of July he became upset and was inconsolable. He was guided to return to the source of his fears and talked of a past life as a black soldier, killed in battle during the American Civil War. Once these repressed memories were able to surface and be expressed within the safety and security of his current life, they could be released. She tells many similar stories in her books about children with unresolved emotions, trauma and fears from other lifetimes who have been cured of these debilitating conditions by talking about their past life experiences. Mostly it's just enough for them to remember and to share what happened. Sometimes the child needs to revisit and re-experience the intense emotions before healing can occur. I experienced this firsthand when, as a five year old, my son relived the terrors of his most recent past life—in the 1970s in Cambodia during the Pol Pot regime.

Just as we carry issues from childhood into our adult lives, we carry unresolved baggage from past lifetimes into our new incarnations. Each new life brings a fresh opportunity to address these. Our soul's aim is for us to become whole and healed and it is always guiding us from a higher vantage point in the best direction for our growth.

The founder of psychoanalysis, Sigmund Freud, discovered the power of helping his patients remember repressed memories from childhood. Once these were unearthed and brought into the light of day a catharsis or healing took place. This is a central idea of psychotherapy. This process works and I believe regression therapy is an extension of this. It takes the process one step further by tapping into old memories and traumas that are stored in our bodies and energy fields. Not only do we hold unconscious memories from our current lifetime but we carry subconscious memories from previous lifetimes as well. These repressed memories govern our behaviour, drive some of our deepest fears and in many cases are behind the mental and physical dis-eases we suffer from.

Many of the 'mentally ill' patients I have met since my daughter became unwell have experiences of family dysfunction, trauma, abuse and violence and their conditions are understandable in light of their life experiences. There are exceptions, however. I believe that, for many, mental illness is a soul sickness where sufferers carry repressed memories of trauma, violence and abuse that occurred in other incarnations. The Akashic Records cast a new light on Post Traumatic Stress Disorder, which is one of Alice's diagnoses. There is no doubt that she is affected by this. However she carries the trauma from many lifetimes, not just this one.

I have found evidence of this in my work in the Records, and these ideas are substantiated by author Robert Schwartz. In his books, *Your Soul's Plan* and *Your Soul's Gift*, he discusses the soul reasons for life challenges faced by real subjects. He uses the abilities of several channels able to connect with the soul and gives an expansive view of his subjects' life plans and the higher reasons for their chosen paths. In *Your Soul's Gift,* Robert writes about those who are facing specific life challenges, such as mental illness. Schwartz supports the view that past life trauma is a contributor to mental instability and gives the example of, Mikaela, a woman who has chosen mental illness to bring about deep soul healing.

It is time for those who work with the mentally and physically ill to realise the limitations of the old paradigm and to open up to a wider perspective where a belief in reincarnation is a central tenet and which takes into account the impact of past life experiences.

One day I received a call from a woman named Joy who was cautious and asked a myriad of questions. She decided she would like a reading which I conducted by email. Joy has been diagnosed with Bipolar Disorder and has found life challenging. She has had few Earth lives and has a soul history of suicide. She consciously chose to return to Earth at this time to repay karma and to give her soul the opportunity for healing and completion. When she planned this life it was decided she would develop a mental illness. This would give her the best opportunity for soul growth, would force her to face circumstances similar to those she had not overcome in previous lives and prepare her for her life mission to help the mentally ill and disadvantaged:

> *These feelings that life is too hard and of wanting to die are not new to you. You have had them in every incarnation you have had on Earth and have acted on them in several. In*

this lifetime your plan is to manage and gain control over these feelings and to assist others who struggle in this way.

From Joy's Akashic Record it was obvious she had come into this life carrying considerable trauma:

You are a highly evolved soul who has had few Earth lives, all of which have been traumatic. You were reluctant to come to Earth but you had to address and clear some karmic issues before planetary Ascension took place. You left it until the last moment. On a soul level you knew it was in your best interests to complete your series of incarnations on this planet.

Joy asked what had caused her Bipolar Disorder, and this was her answer:

This was a genetic choice. You chose to be born into a family where the gene pool held this possibility. This is also an illness many people have who are open to psychic energy and find it difficult to manage. You are wide open spiritually and like a magnet to shadow or darker energies that gather around you like moths to a flame. There is a huge difference between who you are when you are fully aligned with your soul self and wisdom and who you are when you are the focus of interference from negative entities and energies. They are attracted by your light and, because of your sensitivity, easily gain entrance and disturb your thoughts. The negative thoughts are not yours but they activate the soul memories of some of the difficult lives you have experienced and can bring you down.

Joy asked what she needed to do to heal her mental condition The response was:

You can heal from it completely. The first step is to protect yourself at all times. Medication will weaken your energy field and allow the negative energies and thoughts to enter. You could benefit from taking alternative and non-chemical supplements and vitamins. Soul retrieval work and regular energy healing would help as well as continuing on your path of spiritual enlightenment. When you are fully aligned with your soul self and 'I AM' presence you will be healed.

Since this reading three years ago, the transformation in Joy has been astounding! She has bravely and determinedly forged on, seeking healing and making the most of opportunities to grow and develop spiritually. She is now off all medication and is writing a book to help and inspire others, particularly the so-called 'mentally ill.' I last saw Joy in the beautiful Coromandel area of New Zealand. She had finished a retreat, booked in for a second and was glowing, radiant and joyful for the first time (she told me) in her life.

Louise Hay, in *You Can Heal Your Life*, her pioneering work on the mind/body connection, has related unexpressed feelings to every physical malady. It is high time we recognised the spiritual component of 'mental illness' and understood the impact on the mind of unresolved and repressed memories, trauma and experiences from other lifetimes. If we suffer a traumatic death we carry the memory, fears and anxieties into our next lifetime. Just as an abused child is hurt and their adult life is affected, if we have experienced past life trauma our fragile psyche is damaged. Mental conditions are often a sickness of the soul which can only be healed at a soul level.

It is useful to have an overview through the Akashic Records and to be able to identify some of the distorted beliefs we have had throughout time. Most of us have some degree of past life trauma and many children are affected by it. There are always good reasons for the ways people behave. A clingy child, the fear of abandonment, fear or phobia of water, fire, starvation and death (to name but a few) often have their roots in a past life. By drawing out the specific fear, the memory of being left, drowned, burned to death or dying of starvation can be released and healed and the person freed from its after effects.

Eve asked me about her relationship with her four year old son, Cory. He was very attached to her and was only happy when she was near. If she left him, even to go into the next room, he would scream. Eve admitted that she was over-protective and had a fear of losing him. She told me that while she had been happy to send her other children on a holiday with their grandmother, she had kept Cory at home. Through Eve's Akashic Record I found that in a former life, also as mother and son, she had left him when she went away to gather food and had been kidnapped and never returned. This scenario made sense to Eve and helped her deal with Cory so he felt safe. It also helped her to let go of her fears about her son. He is now happy and secure without his mother and recently went overseas with his brothers, sisters and grandmother.

A client who asked why she has a fear of failing her family received this reply:

> *This is a past life fear from a difficult life in Ireland during the potato famine. You were a widow and the mother of a large family whom you lost one by one through malnutrition, starvation and disease. You had only one surviving child in that life. It was heartbreaking for you to lose your children in this slow and agonising way. Although it wasn't your fault, you blamed yourself and still carry the pain and the fear that it could happen again. You also have other lifetimes where you feel you have failed your children.*

Another client with a fear of failure as well as a phobia of birds and water asked about these:

> *These fears originate in past lives. You starved to death in a nomadic life. You were living in a tribe during a drought. The tribal elders had talked of a waterhole that could be found by*

following the moon and certain star formations. The survival of your people was at stake and with two others you volunteered to try to find this legendary oasis. You were unsuccessful and had to watch as your companions died and were eaten by vultures.

Your last memories in this lifetime were of lying dehydrated and delirious, watching the birds circling. You knew that they represented death and felt huge despair. You knew you would die and that so would your tribesmen. You felt you had failed and were responsible for their fate. That is where your fear of birds comes from and it is also linked to your fear of failure.

You have drowned in two lifetimes. In one you drowned as a 'witch.' You were a healer and a person who could see and feel things that others couldn't. You used this to help people in your community. You were branded a witch and subjected to a test you couldn't possibly survive. You were weighed down with rocks and thrown into a river. If you lived you would be confirmed as a witch and killed ... and if you drowned, would be proven innocent. You also died in a flood many lifetimes ago. You were a child who was swept away by a swollen river.

Another client, Bridget, has brought disturbing memories from previous lifetimes into this one. She admits she has a strong need to be in control of her life and others. I was able to tell her:

You have soul trauma relating to lifetimes that ended when things spiralled out of control. There have been incidents in this lifetime such as the death of your sister and the birth of your children which have triggered these memories and brought this aspect of yourself to the fore. This desire to be in control is a trait you have chosen to work with in this lifetime and you are making good progress. It is at its strongest when you are feeling tired and overwhelmed. It is not who you really are, but is a part of you that you are aware of and are learning to tame. It relates to some past lives that ended in a sudden and traumatic way.

In your immediate past life as a young child you were torn from your mother's arms in the Holocaust and beaten to death. This was an horrific experience and the energetic vibration of this has remained with you. One minute you were cradled by your mother and the next you were brutally murdered. This was a short but happy life until its last moments. You had a loving and devoted mother and the end of this life was in sharp contrast to its beginning, which made it even more traumatic.

Bridget also worried that her relationship with her husband was affected by a fear she had of intimacy and violence and a mistrust of her husband and men in general. As we discovered:

Again, this relates to past life trauma that is affecting you at the moment as a result of the buildup of energies and intensity on the planet and also because when you are tired and your guard is down these feelings easily re-surface. You have been sexually abused in past lifetimes. You were sacrificed in Peru many years ago. A beautiful young girl and a virgin, you were killed on the full moon to appease the gods. Before this happened you were raped by the male leaders of the village. These feelings are re-emerging. They are coming up to be released. They have everything to do with what has happened before and nothing to do with your current relationship. You are going through some intense past life clearing.

The energies in recent years (as we move closer to the 'shift' of the Earth's vibration from the Third to the Fifth Dimension) have, for many people, intensified the process of clearing and healing limiting beliefs and past life memories. For sensitive souls like Bridget with many life experiences behind her, this process has been unrelenting. It has sometimes been difficult, for them, to tell where one life has ended and another has begun. Part of this process of releasing has involved reliving and re-experiencing the feelings and pain of the past. Bridget has felt trapped in a time warp as the emotions, fears, beliefs, and sometimes glimpses and visions of past lives have resurfaced and she has felt as if she is going mad. This 'bleed-through' from past lives and experiences is affecting many of us. It doesn't help that these feelings become stronger as we are letting them go. For Bridget this process has been especially intense because she has lived many challenging lives and because, if she chooses, she has a special purpose in the future to help those suffering from past life trauma. For the sensitive and highly evolved among us it has sometimes been difficult to distinguish between our current and past realities.

Bridget has suffered from depression in this lifetime and admits that she sometimes has irrational thoughts that don't mesh with her experience as a much loved wife and mother. Bridget has a soul history of abuse and mistreatment by men and has found it difficult to trust them. She has projected many unhealed feelings and beliefs from her distant past onto her present-day husband who is a soul mate who loves her and has come in to help her heal this issue. In answer to her question, "What can I learn from my relationship with my husband?" I got the following:

To trust men. He can be trusted. He loves you and there is no negative karma between you. You have been together before as close friends and siblings. There is a close soul connection and he is here to help you learn to trust men again. You have some deep soul wounding from abusive treatment in past lifetimes and this needs to be healed and released. Your husband has offered to assist in this process.

It helps to be aware of how feelings and emotional residue from past lives can interfere with our present day relationships. Like

Alice, Bridget has been reliving past emotional pain in order to let it go.

My friend, Donna, has been experiencing past life trauma and 'bleed-through' by feeling physical pain from past lives. She has found this process particularly acute in recent years. She will suddenly develop severe pain in a part of her body, as painful, she says, as the real thing and will get an impression in her mind of an episode from a past life. Here she describes a recent experience the night before she was to give an important talk on environmental issues:

> *Last night I had another cellular memory clearing experience. I'd gone to bed when I suddenly had a terrible pain in my back. No matter how I positioned myself I couldn't get relief. I became aware that I had a stake through my back. I realised it was a cellular memory related to speaking out, from a life where I was staked (literally) and killed because I spoke up. After about ten minutes, I managed to clear this completely—basically by telling my body that I was no longer afraid of speaking my truth.*

Donna finished her description with:

> *It was really intense pain. My breathing went straight into distress, exactly as it would if this was for real. To me this is an indicator that it is real cellular memory.*

The process of 'bleed-through' is affecting us all as we raise our vibration, as the veil between the spirit and human realities thins and we step from the Third Dimension into the Fifth. Each cell of our body is imprinted with the memories of our soul experiences. As Donna discovered, if talked to directly and respectfully, our cells will work with us to heal physical and emotional pain.

The energy of the New Earth is activating our cell/soul wisdom and past life trauma is impacting on our present-day lives. This merging of the past with the present, is taking many of us out of centre. Acutely sensitive and wide-open, this process is happening more intensely for many with mental conditions and for those like my daughter, Alice, who carry deep soul trauma.

Having access to the Akashic Records is invaluable because it not only allows us to see the bigger picture, but is a place where we can release our pain with ease and grace. Understanding that what is happening is for our highest good and is a necessary part of our Ascension path makes it easier to go with the flow, to blend with the energies and to survive them.

Chapter 11
Clearing and releasing

For the 'old souls' of Earth and the sensitive ones, the last few years have been difficult as we have been relentlessly assaulted by successive bombardments of higher frequency energy which have laid us bare and activated and challenged us on a core, soul level. This has been necessary for the starseeds to deal with the karmic miasma, soul trauma and negative beliefs that have been part of their journey since incarnating on earth. Our sensitivity and receptivity as well as our unique DNA composition has meant that we have been the first to experience this alchemy of mind, body and soul. It has not been an easy road. At times we have felt we have lost our grip on reality but it is a path that has been necessary to prepare us for the 'service work' we came to Earth to do; to assist humanity into the light and to help create a new world order of peace, love and unity.

Alice is a special and sensitive soul and it is my belief that much of her suffering as a young adult has been caused by this process. It has been more extreme in her case because she has experienced severe trauma in a number of lifetimes and has carried a very strong vibration of fear which has coloured her life experience. She is a soul who has not only elected to deal with her own stuff but has agreed to clear karmic debris and limitation along her ancestral family line and from the collective consciousness of humanity.

For Alice, the last seven years have been intense. We have

watched as she has become someone we no longer recognise re-enacting a series of traumatic lives from her past. She has soul themes of being sacrificed, raped, killed, imprisoned, tortured, starved and abandoned. In accessing her Akashic Record I have found that most of the trauma in other lifetimes occurred around the ages of 16-18 which is when she became seriously unwell in this lifetime. At this age in different lifetimes she has been sacrificed to the heavens and to men to advance her family's fortunes, sexually abused, locked up, starved and raped in the Holocaust and has lost her mind.

In recent years the psychiatric ward has become her prison. As a young woman in her current life, she has been raped and has inflicted on herself and replayed some of the worst scenes from her many lifetimes through acts of severe self-harm, suicide attempts and as a sufferer of anorexia. These are the effects of past life trauma at its worst.

As with everything we experience there is a higher reason for it. As our family emerges from the darkness of the last seven years an understanding of the soul reasons for this crisis is helping us to see and appreciate its gifts.

This process has been intense for Alice and those like her who have many lifetimes of trauma on Earth to clear. Andrea, the sister of a friend of mine had been unhappy for years and had always felt like she didn't deserve to belong to her birth family. In her words she felt "unwanted" and like the "black sheep." I found that she shared her most recent past life with some of the members of her current family. They lived in China during the Japanese occupation from the late 1930s—early 1940s where she was again a female, the sixth child of peasants:

These feelings are a carry-over from past lives and in particular a recent life which was short, painful and traumatic. You were unwelcome, an inconvenience and another mouth to feed. As a sensitive soul you picked up on the emotions and feelings around you and made them your own. You felt your family's unhappiness and lack of food was somehow your fault. Your parents in that lifetime were not naturally unkind but faced incredible hardship. They already had five children they could not look after and you added to their burden. It was wartime and there was little food and no way of earning money. You found this life increasingly unbearable. You were the third daughter in the family and felt you were dispensable.

In that lifetime Andrea's oldest brother, who everyone adored, died of an illness contracted because of his weakened and emaciated state. This had disastrous consequences for the sensitive Andrea:

You became a scapegoat after this and felt that everyone wished you had died instead. At the age of seven it all became too much and you killed yourself by drowning in the river. Your family were very upset but it was too late.

Through accessing Andrea's Akashic Record I discovered she had a pattern of withdrawing and isolating herself—a soul history as an outcast who was unable to trust others or feel she deserved to be part of the group. The reasons for this were traced back to a key lifetime:

This desire for isolation and feeling of being different and not trusting others goes a long way back to the destruction of Atlantis. You knew what was happening and what was likely to happen but didn't warn people. You were the daughter of a man who experimented with 'Black Magic' and who misused his power and crystal energy to destroy the continent. You lost your life but as you died berated yourself for not speaking up. If you had you felt the cataclysm may have been avoided.

You have carried feelings of guilt, shame, self-blame and self-judgment ever since and the energy and vibration of these feelings and beliefs has attracted persecution in subsequent lifetimes.

The reverberations from this key lifetime and the emotions it evoked are still being felt by Andrea in her current life and in recent years have intensified making her feel stuck and powerless. To her question, "Why do I find it so difficult to forgive and forget? "I received this answer:

You have been hurt in so many lifetimes by so many people that you find it difficult to trust and to forgive others. We are shedding our '3D' skins and this is bringing up long buried emotions and pain from past lifetimes.

There are many good reasons why you hold a grudge. Some of the people you find hard to forgive have hurt you not only in this lifetime but in others as well. The pain runs very deep. You have the memories of trauma from past lives to release and have chosen some very challenging circumstances and difficult experiences to trigger this process. When you are dealing with concentrated pain from many lifetimes it can be excruciating.

The incoming high vibration energy is accelerating the process of clearing and releasing. In Andrea's case it has aligned with her soul to help her let go of this pattern.

You have become stuck as these feelings from other lifetimes have been emerging in recent years. The Fifth Dimension is higher and lighter and is where your soul resides. The Third Dimension is more dense and fear based. Your human self is stuck in this vibration while your soul self is firmly rooted in the higher energy. This has made life difficult for you. Your soul is drawing experiences to you so you can release what has been holding you back but it is difficult for your human self to let this go particularly if you don't understand what is happening.

Andrea's Akashic Record revealed that like many of us her soul's plan was that she be rewarded with 'work' that would bring her joy and enable her to share her unique gifts and wisdom with others:

Your highest plan is that you will one day help others who are on the fringes of society to feel self-worth and to create lives where they can make a meaningful contribution.

Cheryl is another soul who has had an arduous and painful journey since coming to Earth from Andromeda a long time ago. She has accumulated much trauma which she has been working in recent years to clear. This has been difficult for her but she is coming through it and is now ready to step into her soul destiny.

You were one of those brave souls who left behind the comfort and higher consciousness of the Star Nations and agreed to travel to Earth to experience all facets of the human experience. This has involved many lifetimes of struggle, persecution and difficulty. Along the way you have experienced the darkness as well as the light and have picked up many beliefs that have limited and sabotaged you. You have repeated negative patterns and on a human level your progress has, at times, appeared to be slow.

You have been undergoing an intense process of karmic clearing and releasing. You have lived in fear in many lifetimes and have carried this vibration. This has made your transition difficult. As a part of the harrowing initiation you have been undergoing in recent years you have been tested around fear and now much of what you used to fear has been transmuted into love for both yourself and humanity.

As with Andrea, I found that the fear and limiting beliefs Cheryl carries originated from a lifetime in Atlantis where she had soul abilities as a healer and alchemist and used these to help others. She was not one of those whose experiments resulted in the destruction of Atlantis but felt guilty by association and has carried that guilt ever since:

You have been an experimenter in other lifetimes. I see you as an alchemist. You brought knowledge from your star heritage and concocted potions that helped people to cast out negativity and to improve their physical health. You knew and understood magic but always used it to benefit others. You were respected and loved in Lemuria and did much to use these powers in a positive way in Atlantis.

You were not one of those who abused these abilities and contributed to the downfall of this continent but you carried their guilt. You died as a result of the misdeeds of other scientists and alchemists and ever since have seen these talents of yours as a bad thing. These gifts have come naturally to you in every lifetime so they have been difficult to suppress.

This information again shows the power of the emotionally charged memories that are with us when we die and how these can be carried through many lifetimes, attracting the same experiences to us repeatedly.

You have continued to use your abilities to help others, with combinations of herbs and other concoctions, but have suffered and been persecuted for it. You have denied the essence of who you are for many hundreds of years and this has reinforced feelings of self-doubt, self-loathing and a lack of self-belief and acceptance. These feelings have attracted some difficult experiences to you.

Cheryl asked about any possible health issues and again there was an obvious link between her physical wellbeing in this life and traumatic experiences in previous lives:

You have a tendency towards stomach complaints or gastro issues. This comes from Atlantis where you found the way your colleagues used their skills for their own selfish and destructive ends difficult to stomach. You have carried this ever since. You need to be careful with what you eat. There is also a possibility of some sinus and chest issues. As you lay dying in Atlantis you found it hard to breathe. These complaints are triggered when you are feeling trapped and as if there is no way out of a situation and when others around you are behaving in dishonest and unethical ways.

Since this lifetime in Atlantis, Cheryl has suffered great soul trauma and hardship. The intensity of her clearing process in recent years has reflected her difficult journey but is also an indicator of her immense soul potential and the magnificent possibilities she has in this lifetime.

You have been carrying shame since Atlantis. It is important that you now reconnect with and embrace your galactic heritage so you can be of service to others at this time. You have a special role to play.

Cheryl's story is similar to that of many starseeds who after many years in limbo are finally stepping back into their soul power and beauty and who in the energy of the New Earth will be able to make their own unique and vital contribution.

As a result of what you have gone through your soul wisdom has been activated and is ready to be accessed to help yourself and others. The high vibration energy that is coming in is working on the cells of your body to draw out your soul knowledge and gifts. They are rising to the surface and are ready to be used.

In this lifetime Cheryl's plan is to use her extraordinary talents and soul experiences to not only pull the fields of science and spirituality closer together but to bring planet Earth into closer alignment with her galactic neighbours.

You have much wisdom and knowledge that can be used to make a difference in the field of science. You have a unique contribution to make in bridging the gap between the scientific and the spiritual. You will help scientists see that they are not alone and that they have support and assistance in the higher realms and from other parts of the galaxy.

There is much we can learn from these beings who are working with mankind on breakthroughs in the fields of science and technology.

Cheryl has suffered greatly in many lifetimes, this one included, but as with Alice and with all of us, her soul has been holding a higher vision all along.

As with Cheryl and Andrea, a common theme among my clients is of a traumatic experience in a pivotal lifetime, a defining moment where there was a loss of innocence and where they took on beliefs that they have carried with them ever since. Beliefs like:

» It is not safe to be me.

» Speaking up causes suffering.

» It is all my fault.

» I cannot trust.

» I always lose those I love.

These constructs are limiting and many of us have experienced life after life of shutting ourselves down and denying who we really are. All these lifetimes of 'same old, same old' have literally been soul destroying. Over time this has become unbearable and this influx of energies which are helping us to 're-member' is bringing things to a head.

Another client is highly successful in a traditional sense. She has worked her way to the top of her profession, has a well paid job and all the trappings of success. When she contacted me she was finding the job she once loved, and which had given her stability through a marriage breakup and other personal upheavals, no longer fulfilling. She told me she felt as if she had shut down her light. I found that this is exactly what had happened. She had an impressive soul heritage as a teacher, a healer and a High Priestess in the Temple of Isis but all this had changed after a lifetime during the time of Christ. A member of the Essene community, she had witnessed the Crucifixion and then, as a follower of Jesus, been killed. She had closed down after this to protect herself from further pain and had stopped listening to her soul.

She had been playing it safe and had had many lifetimes of 'going through the motions.' This had become increasingly unbearable and that is why she contacted me. Her challenge in this lifetime is to overcome her fears and to follow her heart. She is planning to resign from her job; the rewards, if she does break this pattern will be great. The plan is for her to reconnect with the highest expression of herself and to work helping others to overcome their fears and find joy and meaning in their lives. This will not only be healing for her but for those she works with.

I have helped clients to heal painful memories in past life regressions but can do this more easily through accessing their Akashic Records. By sharing information about traumatic events I can help them to let the memories go. Sometimes just telling the story is enough. I can see when what I am saying resonates with someone because there will be a strong emotional reaction. I love it when my clients cry! Crying during a reading is good. It is a sign that the truth is rising to the surface.

Sometimes I need to help release a memory by taking my client back in time. I ask them to close their eyes and, invoking their

higher-self, guides, various **Ascended Masters** and **Archangels**, help them to put the past incident in perspective, to forgive themselves (and others involved if necessary) and to let it go and move on.

I also work within the Akashic Records to access the subconscious mind and to help clients to release and clear limiting and sabotaging thoughts, beliefs, feelings, patterns and past life trauma from the cells of their physical bodies and the atoms and molecules of their etheric bodies. Greg Braden and Bruce Lipton have both written about the power of the subconscious mind and of our early life programming. They say that children's experiences in the first seven years lay down the template for their lives. What happens to them may not be consciously remembered but the memories are stored in the subconscious.

Braden says that our subconscious mind holds the memory of every experience we have ever had in our lives, our thoughts about them and our subsequent beliefs. Our subconscious mind doesn't think, it reacts and is responsible for upwards of 90 percent of our actions. This, he says, explains why it is so difficult to change and to rid ourselves of negative programming. He gives scientific evidence to show how the resonance and the vibration of our programmed beliefs is carried in the energy matrix surrounding our bodies. Lipton has proven through his research that our subconscious beliefs are held at a cellular level.

The late Dolores Cannon, in her past life regression sessions, worked with the storehouse of wisdom that is our subconscious mind. Aligned with our soul truth and with its reservoir of memories she found that this part of our mind knows what is best for us.

Before working with a client, Dolores got to know them, making notes on what they wanted to find out and any healing that needed to take place. A typical session involved taking a client into a hypnotic trance, into a past life with direct relevance to their current one and then connecting with the 'subconscious' of the individual for clarification on other issues. I trained with Dolores and have used this method and can verify that our subconscious memory goes way beyond our present lifetime. Lipton and Braden have proved that we carry the core beliefs from childhood in our bodies and energy fields. I agree with them but believe that we also carry memories and beliefs from previous lifetimes.

If our subconscious memories account for over 90 percent of our actions, it is easy to see, when we are affected by so many experiences we can't consciously remember, why it has been difficult for us to overcome our self-defeating behaviours. The good news is that after many lifetimes of being in the grip of forces seemingly beyond our control and being pulled back into a maelstrom of despair, help is at hand! The Akashic Records is the perfect place for us to understand and to release all that has been holding us back.

In 2014 I had an unexpected trip to attend my nephew's wedding celebrations in Vienna. As it had been thirty years since I was last in Europe and it is so far away I decided to stay on for three weeks and travel from Vienna to the Czech Republic, through Poland and Germany and back to Austria again. I travelled on a Eurail Pass with my sister who gave me free rein with the itinerary. As I planned the trip I didn't realise that my soul was in charge. It prompted me to travel to some intense locations. We visited Lidice in the Czech Republic, the Jewish Museum in Prague, Auschwitz-Birkenau in Poland and Buchenwald in Germany.

I went to these places with my Akashic Record open, which in retrospect was asking for trouble, but was guided on a soul level to do this. I said some prayers for Alice at Auschwitz and forgave myself at Buchenwald which, I confess, was hauntingly familiar.

I arrived back feeling really weird and promptly got sick. It was more than jetlag. Some deep cellular clearing had been triggered. I travelled through familiar territory, to some past life haunts. Not surprisingly the visits to concentration camps affected me greatly. I knew I had to go to these places ... not because of a human need but to meet the needs of my soul who saw it as an opportunity for some deep clearing and healing. I have been through this many times in recent years and it is never easy. Once it is over I feel lighter and know I have had an upgrade in vibration. I am grateful to Alice as my experiences with her have accelerated this process. It is easier now I have discovered the Akashic Records as once I recover from my initial disorientated state I am able to use them to help myself.

Our lifetimes on Earth have been like a very long train journey. We have covered many miles and disembarked at many stations. At our different stop off points (lifetimes) we have picked up beliefs, behaviours, thoughts and fears that have ground us down and kept us stuck. Those of us who come from the stars have carried a higher vibration and have been an easy target for persecution and the projections of fear from those around us. For most starseeds our current lifetime has been a challenging one especially in recent years as we have been letting go of lifetimes of limitation from our cellular memory and energy field.

To do this in the 'old energy' we have had to relive and re-experience the feelings and pain in order to let them go. This process can be agonising and when the feelings and memories are coming up to be released the intensity of our emotions can be overwhelming.

Like the contractions of labour, this letting go has come in waves. In between each cycle we feel fine but each time the pain returns it is crushing and debilitating. It is worth it in the end because once it is over we emerge reborn.

When I work to remove this stuck energy I use the power of words. In his experiments with water, the late Masuru Emoto showed that words hold a distinct vibration. He wrote positive and negative words on separate pieces of paper, attached them to containers of water and froze them. When looking at this ice under a microscope the difference between the crystalline formations was startling. The structure of the ice with the positive word attached looked beautiful through his lense while the molecular structure in the container marked by the negative word was jagged and discordant.

For years one of my favourite sayings as a parenting teacher was Nathaniel Branden's, 'words linger long and poisonously.' I made a point of emphasising the harm parents can do to their children through words and how damaging negative core beliefs can be. In light of Emoto's experiments and given that our bodies are 50-75 percent water, we can see how verbal abuse can not only affect us emotionally but physiologically. The realisation that many of us have carried negative beliefs with us from lifetime to lifetime gives new meaning to Brandon's phrase!

During healing sessions with clients I help them release, clear and heal from negative programming they have acquired in other lifetimes. Many of us have a 'water-shed' lifetime that ended in a traumatic way. Our limiting beliefs are almost always taken on at the moment of death. If we die suddenly and unexpectedly they leave a powerful energetic imprint which if reactivated in a subsequent incarnation can draw the same experiences back to us. Many old souls hold negative beliefs within their cells and in the **morphogenetic** fields surrounding their bodies and have become locked in a self-perpetuating cycle of sabotage and difficulty.

Some of these most common beliefs are:

» I am not good enough.

» I am a failure.

» Life is a struggle.

» I deserve to suffer.

» It is all my fault.

» I can't trust.

» I will never amount to anything.

» Nobody wants me.

» It is not safe to love.

Imran felt stuck and as if his thoughts were holding him back. He admitted that he felt very much 'in his head' and asked about this tendency. I found that he originated as a soul in Alpha Centauri and had agreed to come to earth 150,000 years ago as a scout or forerunner for the larger group of starseeds who came in later. Alpha Centauri is a star whose inhabitants understand the power of the mind to create and manifest and these abilities come naturally to Imran:

> *Your soul heritage on Alpha Centauri has emphasised the importance of the mind and the power of beliefs in creating our reality. You know how easy it is to manifest and have brought in with you the innate knowledge of how to do this in a way that not only engages the mind but the heart. If you choose, this is what you will learn how to do and teach to others.*

> *Your human aspect and conditioning has further reinforced this natural tendency to be locked in by your limiting core beliefs. Your experiences in this lifetime and indeed in your other lifetimes on Earth have kept you in your head. Many of the beliefs you carry come from these other lifetimes and were reactivated and strengthened by the experiences you had early on in this one.*

I discovered that, as is usually the case, Imran's life purpose was directly linked to his current life experience. Imran's soul plan in this lifetime is for him to teach others how to use their head and heart to create what they want. I found that trauma experienced in previous lives, especially his most recent past life, was holding him back:

> *You have had comparatively few lifetimes here but chose to have two very close together. You were here during World War II and experienced extreme trauma as a Jewish boy who was experimented on by the Nazis. As a result of this experience and those from other Earth lifetimes, your heart shut down. You put an energetic, protective coating over it to stop yourself from being hurt. You were an innocent, trusting boy who was used as a guinea pig. You agreed to take part in an experiment many years ago as a starseed who came to Earth but you only consented to the Nazi experiments under duress. You carry some beliefs which still affect and limit you:*

> » *I am worthless.*

> » *Life is a struggle.*

> » *I am different and don't fit in.*

> *The protective coating around your heart needs to be removed and some work done on the soul trauma you carry. This will remove all barriers and you will then be guided to manifest and create through thought from a head and heart space. You have the knowledge within to integrate the two in this way and to more powerfully manifest your dreams and desires. The plan is for you to do this in your own life and then to teach this to others. The blend of head, heart and the new Fifth Dimensional energy will be a powerful one and will work magic and create miracles in your life and in the lives of those you work with.*

I was able to help Imran to remove the protective coating around his heart and to free him from the beliefs that had been stopping him from moving forward.

My friend, Amelia, has had a very hard life. She has shared some of her story with me but says there is much more to tell. Her life has been a series of crises that began before she was born!

Her mother, a single parent of two boys, met and fell in love with Amelia's father. Persuasive and charming he encouraged her to sell her possessions and to give him her money so he could take the family to the US to start a new life. Heavily pregnant with Amelia, she packed her bags, said goodbye to family and friends and waited with her excited sons for the taxi to the airport to arrive. It didn't come and neither did her boyfriend.

Amelia's earliest memories are of crying in her cot and waiting for her mother to pick her up. As she grew up she was small for her age and lived in a tough part of town where she never felt safe. Walking to the corner shop to buy food was an ordeal. There were two gangs, one at each end of her street, who would attack her, taking her money and groceries. Her neighbourhood was an 'urban jungle' and her home wasn't safe either. From an early age she was subjected to sexual abuse from a male mentor to her older brothers.

Since then the pressure has been unrelenting as she has faced one challenge after another. Among other things Amelia, now in her late forties, has been discharged as bankrupt, diagnosed with thyroid cancer, been in a succession of unhealthy and sometimes violent relationships, joined and left a religious sect and experienced many difficulties with her children. For years she has been plagued by nightmares. She says this life has been one long nightmare. In Amelia's words:

"I've been through lots of lifetimes in one. There are many times I could have committed suicide. I'm still here. I'm not going to give up ever. I have battled every step of the way."

Only a highly evolved being would take on such difficulty. Amelia's Akashic Record confirmed that she is an old and special soul:

You have chosen a challenging start to life to set you up for the future which will more than make up for your struggles. You are a starseed who was a much revered and gifted teacher/ healer in ancient Lemuria. You were a soul who originated in the star system of the Pleiades and chose to come to Earth to help bring in the light. You held this light at first but over time it dimmed as you experienced lives of hardship, suffering and persecution.

All her life she has felt very alone and has been haunted by a fear of loss. I traced these feelings back to a lifetime in Pompeii in Italy when Mt Vesuvius erupted.

You carry a deep belief that you don't deserve happiness. You have carried this through many lifetimes and now it is time to let it go. This belief originated in a lifetime in the Italian town of Pompeii. You were young, beautiful and happy. You had a difficult childhood where you were neglected and practically lived on the streets. Your life had a dramatic turn around when you were taken in by a wealthy couple and raised as their own. You grew up and met and fell in love with an eligible young man and produced three beautiful children. When the eruption of Mt Vesuvius occurred your children were at home with a servant. You were at the local bath house. Your house and your children were in the direct path of the molten magma and you lost both home and family. You survived but were devastated and felt you were to blame.

The early feelings you had in that lifetime of being worthless and unlovable came back and you have held the belief that you don't deserve happiness ever since and the conviction that when

*things go well for you it will not last and you will eventually lose
everything.*

In many subsequent lifetimes, Amelia has recreated her
experiences in Pompeii in one form or another. The purpose of the
first part of her current life has been to free herself from the residue
and damaging imprints of these lives.

*This life has been very difficult for you as you have had huge
trauma from past lives to deal with as well as their associated
limiting beliefs, fears, sabotaging patterns and uncomfortable
feelings. Each emotional upheaval and challenge has helped
you to release and let go of another layer of pain and heartache.
You have been letting go in the oldest and most difficult way by
recreating experiences and reliving the pain.*

*You have chosen a very tough road to prepare you for your
future work. It was thought that going to the depths and feeling
the full intensity of human suffering would help you empathise
and connect from the heart with the many you will help.*

I gave Amelia the tools to work within her Akashic Record to
release these beliefs and memories and to bring in new and more
affirming ones. For example:

I deserve the best life has to offer.

I grow and evolve through joy not pain.

*I transform my life with ease and grace and help others to
do the same.*

Amelia's life and experiences have been the perfect preparation
for the soul work she is destined to do:

*Part of your journey is to learn that there are easier ways
to release the past and to let go of trauma. The energy of your
trauma is held at a cellular and an energetic level in and*

around your body and there are painless ways of releasing it. You are nearly there. Your highest potential for this lifetime is to be a lifeline to people in despair. To prepare you for this task you have had to experience the depths of despair yourself.

Amelia asked me about her work in the future. I replied:

This will come to you soon. You have had a difficult life with much to learn and to clear. You are near the end of the road and nearly at your destination. There are many people for you to help in the future.

Take one step towards your vision every day. Somewhere on your journey, you will find you have all you have ever wanted and that you have regained love and respect for yourself. This is your most important purpose in this lifetime (apart from the service work you will do) and it is necessary before you can fully love and assist others.

Recently I heard from a very excited Amelia. After years of difficulty she had at last experienced joy in her life and a brief taste of her life's work. She was ecstatic and hungry for more. A friend had visited unexpectedly with a very unhappy teenage girl. By the end of the visit both Amelia and the young woman had been transformed. As Amelia told me:

The other day a young girl who was very depressed ended up at my house ... I was able to relate closely to her and to connect at a very deep level. She felt the sincerity of my energy and we transferred healing to each other. It was very special. Because of my own life experiences I am able to understand how light can shine so brightly against the darkness. For the first time in my life I felt passion and purpose. I have such a strong desire to do this work ... to pull others out of the pit I have been stuck in.

Like Amelia and Alice, clearing and releasing is a big part of what we signed up for in this lifetime. On a human level this can be hell on Earth but from a soul perspective it is necessary to prepare and motivate us for our soul assignments. Throughout this modern day initiation process we must make ourselves our number one priority for it is this inner work and focus that will make it possible for us to help many people in the future.

Chapter 12
Healing in the Akashic Records

The Akashic Records are not only a repository of information, they are a healing place. Early on in my work I was guided to facilitate healing within the sacred space of the Records. Clients reported that magical synchronicities and events occurred after their sessions. I felt energised after each appointment and realised that every time I went into the Akashic Records I was benefitting from their pure and high vibration. The Akashic Records are a gateway to healing which I use to help myself and others. Any healing within the Akashic Records is enhanced and amplified by their energy.

If I have several days without being in the Records I notice it. I begin to feel down and old sabotaging habits start to kick in. This work is the answer to my prayers. It is giving me exactly what I need to heal. In this life and in my most recent lifetimes I have been stuck and mired in fear, anxiety, limiting beliefs and ingrained patterns of behaviour. My life purpose this time round is multi-layered but at the core of it is a desire to free myself from a cycle of lifetimes where I have been trapped in negativity and despair and have not realised my potential. This came to a head in my immediate past life where I died a depressed and broken man. I brought these beliefs and tendencies directly into this lifetime. The plan is for me to release and heal these and to reconnect with my soul self, the essence of who I am, and with all the gifts and abilities of my starseed lineage. Working in the Akashic Records is helping with this and I have been utilising their sanctity and power to release in stages what has been holding me back for a very long time. This is still a work in progress, I am a work in progress. I can vouch for the healing vibration of the Akashic Records and am enjoying teaching others the healing techniques I am using on myself in my Soul History workshops.

The last few years, with 'one foot' in the Third and 'one foot' in the Fifth Dimensions, have been a time of turmoil with waves of human limitation from many lifetimes coming up to be released. We are ready to step into our 'new skins' but, like a snake, we have to shed the old one first. This can be painful. I have learned that resistance creates pain and that it is best to go with the flow. The energy of the Akashic Records is helping me do this.

I have known for a while that these healing techniques work but did not understand why. I believe that the energy of the Akashic Records is the same vibration accessed by those who work in other healing modalities. In 1995, Vianna Stibel, the creator of *Theta Healing*, used the healing energies of the neutral theta brainwave state to heal herself from cancer in her leg. The healing was instantaneous and since then she has successfully taught this approach to thousands of people worldwide. Theta healing frees the body of toxic feelings, thoughts and beliefs. This neutral, healing vibration is the energy of the Fifth Dimension and is also the energy of the Akashic Records. In this vibration it is easier than ever to heal ourselves in mind, body and spirit as this energy is connecting with and unlocking the **multi-dimensional** aspects of our DNA. It is the energy of miracles.

Each cell of our body is an intelligent entity. The incoming light and high vibrational energy in recent years is activating the DNA (over 90 percent) which scientists have called 'junk' because under a Third Dimensional microscope it appears to have no use. The Fifth

Dimensional energy is bringing this dormant aspect of our cells to life with all of its quantum potential. The possibilities for healing inherent in this are huge, especially if we connect with the innate wisdom of each cell and communicate and work with it. All human beings now have this 12 strand DNA wiring which connects us to our god-selves (see Chapters 1 and 4). After thousands of years the energy pouring into the planet is bringing this to life. Within our newly activated DNA lies an imprint of our Akashic Record and soul history and it is this I work with to facilitate healing for myself and others. Working within a client's open Akashic Record makes the healing even more powerful. It enables us to find the root cause of an issue and to heal it on a soul level.

The healing process I use is very simple. The most important part is setting the intention which is a request to the Universe for what I or my client would like to happen. I always state this at the beginning. For example, "My intention for this healing is to assist [xxx] to release the belief, "I am not good enough.""

I then access the Akashic Record of my subject to find the origin of this belief. I find out when, where and why it was taken on and relay information about how the belief has had an impact in various lifetimes. I ask **St Germain** to remove the imprint and vibration of the belief, pattern, thought or fear from the cells of the body and my client's energy field. I guide them to talk to their body directly and to ask their cells to let go of the trauma and limitation from their cellular memory. I then bring in the positive to replace what has been taken away and anchor high vibration words and more affirming beliefs in my client's physical and energy bodies. I activate and anchor the vibration of whatever I feel will help such as the energies of harmony, abundance, trust, joy, confidence, self-belief, balance, empowerment, safety or peace or the beliefs," I deserve the best life has to offer" or " It is safe to be me." Lastly, I connect my client to their **Christed Selves**—the part of them that is infused with the **Christ Consciousness energy** which is currently pouring onto the planet and accelerating cellular alchemy.

This is my basic process. I have used it successfully with myself and others. I believe that if an intention is stated and a client fully embraces it and trusts in the outcome it 'has' to happen. Simplicity is the key in the 'new energy' and I am finding the ease and flow with which things can happen, if you 'believe it is possible', refreshing and exciting!

Our core beliefs reinforce patterns of behaviour which we find easy to slot back into. If we have had lifetime after lifetime putting the needs of others first or of being irresponsible for example, it feels natural to do this again, especially if we are living with those we have played this out with before. Continuing these patterns is disempowering not only for us but for others involved in the recurrent drama. It is never for the highest good of anyone to perpetuate or enable unhealthy behaviours. Once you are in the Akashic Records it is easy to see the destructive actions which have echoed along a soul timeline and continue to have an impact. When these have been identified and brought into a client's awareness they are able to let them go.

Common patterns of behaviour I have worked with are:

» Self-sabotage.

» Self-sacrifice (or putting other's needs before your own).

» Helplessness.

» Victimhood.

» Addiction to drama.

» Other addictive behaviours.

» Defensiveness.

» Self-blame.

» People pleasing.

» Rescuing (doing things for others that they can easily do for themselves).

Isla is a young woman who is juggling family commitments and running a business. She has big dreams for her career and her life but feels pulled in many directions and as if she can't do justice to either job. When I went into her Record a pattern of self-sacrifice over many lifetimes emerged:

> *You have strong beliefs about what a good wife and mother does and doesn't do. This has been your conditioning and comes from past life experiences where you have sacrificed your own needs and been literally sacrificed to meet the needs of others. This is a pattern you have been locked into for many lifetimes. It is time for this to stop.*

She asked what was blocking her financial success and this was the reply:

> *As part of this theme of self-sacrifice you have had past lives in religious orders and have taken vows of poverty. They are still affecting you.*

Isla's story got even more interesting when she asked about her relationship with her husband:

> *You have been with your current husband before and there is a karmic link. In a past life he sacrificed you in a 'pagan' ceremony. You were a young woman in South America and there was a drought. The rain didn't come for two seasons. Your tribe*

decided the Gods were angered and that a sacrifice was needed. Your current husband was the tribal leader and you were his daughter. He loved you very much but felt responsible for the situation (he saw the drought as punishment for the slaughter of innocent villagers several years before). He decided he should sacrifice you. You have been with him in other lifetimes where you have sacrificed your needs for his. This pattern between you is deep-seated and is easy to slip back into.

Isla's plan for this lifetime is to step back into her power, to break the pattern of self-sacrifice and to learn and teach others that it is possible to have it all. Her path is one that many of us have walked and will walk in the years to come now we can let go of what has been holding us back. Isla's reading ended on a positive note:

You have been going through a very difficult process, a 'dark night of the soul' that many lightworkers face. As part of this, many of the challenges we haven't managed to overcome in other lifetimes are presented to us so we can learn the lessons we chose to learn and be prepared for the soul service work we came to do. All is on track. You are well on the way to mastery.

Johnny is a 43 year old single man who has packed a wealth of experiences into his life. When he came to me he had just lost everything: his money, his home and his relationship. He also felt he had lost the love and support of his parents and was at a low ebb. I found that he has been repeating a pattern in this lifetime and in others of swinging dramatically between success and failure. He told me there were times in his life when he had experienced meteoric success and times, like now, when he felt an abject failure. I found that at the root of this was the belief, 'Success is always followed by failure.' I worked with him to reframe his belief system and to alter this template so he can fulfil his destiny.

This belief that good times are possible but they never last is one many of my clients have. For most it stems from a life where everything changed suddenly and blew apart (often in Atlantis) and has been reinforced by many lifetimes of human struggle where things have not gone according to plan.

I not only utilise the energy of the Akashic Records to release and re-programme beliefs, negativity and sabotaging patterns of behaviour stored in our subconscious minds but have been guided to assist others with:

» Fears which often have their roots in a past life, such as the fear of rejection, the fear of loss, abandonment, suffering, failure or success ... and also more tangible fears for example, a fear of heights, death, fire or public speaking.

» The release of feelings that are holding them back including self-hatred, self-doubt, shame, guilt, sadness and grief, anxiety, hopelessness, self-judgment, unforgiveness.

» **Soul retrieval.**

» The 'letting go' of past life trauma.

» The clearing and removal of entities, **implants** and **attachments.**

» The cutting of **cords.**

» The balancing of karma.

» Inner child healing and healing within families.

Within the energy of the Akashic Records I have worked with the higher selves of souls to facilitate forgiveness, healing and release.

I do what I am guided to do and every session is different. Working within the Records allows me to effect healing on a deep soul level. The energy of both the Akashic Records and the Fifth Dimension is that anything is possible. It is a 'double whammy' and one in which magic definitely happens!

A well known human response to trauma is **dissociation**. This is where as a result of a traumatic event a person detaches from reality and becomes distant and difficult to reach. As a protective mechanism they shut out the memory of what happened and have no conscious recollection of it. In this process a **soul fragment** splits off from the psyche. If the trauma occurs as a four year old, for example, this piece will carry the fears and the characteristics of a child of this age. This unintegrated **sub-personality** can manifest throughout our lives as child-like behaviour.

When Alice first became unwell, she was often in a dissociative state. For those close to her it was scary seeing the person we loved go AWOL. Her eyes were glazed and sometimes it was as if no one was home. This was, I believe, a reaction to the trauma of being raped at age sixteen, and as I looked back I remembered the same symptoms, the same 'missing in action' stare after she was 'abused' at age four. Something shut down in her after that. From Alice's Akashic Record I have learned that she has suffered in many lifetimes at these same ages.

Sigmund Freud coined the term '**Repetition Compulsion**' to describe the process where we repeatedly draw painful experiences back to us and re-create similar scenarios in an attempt to heal our childhood wounds. Freud talked of this in the context of a single lifetime, but from my work in the Records I have learned, because of our soul's innate desire to heal, that this can occur in a succession of lifetimes. We hold the memories of past life trauma in our bodies which magnetise similar experiences to us over and over again. Alice has been wounded at the ages of four and sixteen in many lifetimes. As a result her four-year old and sixteen-year old aspects have split off repeatedly almost taking on a life of their own.

These sub-personalities can keep sabotaging our progress. They need to work with, not against us so we can move forward in our lives. Alice has come a long way and is now mostly a functioning and responsible adult. When anything happens to trigger deep fear or anger, however, her four and sixteen-year olds are easy to spot and she becomes unsafe and is admitted to hospital. Her four-year old is very sweet. She just wants to be looked after and loved. Her sixteen-year old has attitude and can be rebellious. She can behave in a way she never did as a child, with angry outbursts and self-harming and destructive episodes.

The forgotten four-year old and in particular the furious sixteen-year old can create havoc. In Alice's case many accumulated lifetimes of trauma have, I believe, contributed to the severity of her illness. Not only has she lost soul fragments in this lifetime but in others as well. Alice has allowed me one soul retrieval session and gave me permission to work with her from a distance to reintegrate these soul pieces but she is wary of my efforts. After seven years she is entrenched in the mental health system and the orthodox model for treatment. I get frustrated at times knowing I have skills that could help my daughter and have to remind myself that it is her journey and that on a soul level all is happening as it should.

Healing in the Akashic Records as with any healing is more successful if who we are working with believes it can help them. If the belief isn't there it is not so easy. Soul Retrieval is the process of gathering up soul fragments that have split off as a result of trauma in our current life and in others and reintegrating them into the psyche. It is helpful for everyone especially those who have scattered energy, who have experienced trauma and the so-called mentally ill.

This advice came through for a sufferer of Bipolar Disorder:

Soul retrieval work would be helpful to assist the lost and disowned fragments that have splintered off in your childhood and during various lifetimes to return. This would help to ground and integrate you and to heal you from the Bipolar Disorder which is the physical manifestation of these experiences.

This client was greatly helped by this process and I have used it successfully with clients suffering from anxiety and post-traumatic stress issues.

I had two very powerful sessions with a woman called Clare who was still being strongly affected by a lifetime that ended long ago in a sudden and traumatic way. In her current lifetime Clare has felt alone, unworthy and ashamed of herself and has not known why. She told me she had always felt like 'an outsider' and had found it difficult to trust others. I found that as a young woman in Lemuria, she was taken in by a group of people who were partly responsible for the destruction of the continent. She trusted and believed this group who duped her into passing on information which they later used to destroy Lemuria and its inhabitants.

You don't trust people and with good reason. Your soul experiences have taught you that it is not safe to trust and to 'watch your back.' You have been betrayed many times. The first time was in Lemuria when you were abused by those of the dark who used you to gain important information about the Lemurian priesthood and their ancient knowledge. You were a naive soul then and trusted them completely. You had no idea of their plans or that they would result in the destruction of many people dear to you, an entire civilisation and way of life. You took on beliefs after this disaster which it is now time to release.

Not only did Clare lose her life but she lost many people she loved and as she died she felt that it was all her fault and that she had been responsible for the demise of Lemuria. The beliefs that

Clare took on have echoed down her timeline through subsequent incarnations attracting experiences that have only strengthened her core beliefs of:

- » I am unworthy.

- » I don't deserve friendship and support.

- » It is all my fault.

- » I can't be trusted.

- » I can't trust others.

- » I deserve to be punished.

Clare admitted she constantly judged others and asked about this. I answered her:

Your judgment of others stems from your judgment of yourself. You have been hard on yourself since Lemurian times, beating yourself up for something that was beyond your control. You were no match for the forces of the darkness. They seduced you with lies, deceit, manipulation and flattery and convinced you that you would be helping those of the priesthood and those of the light by giving them information. They used this to set in motion a chain of events that destroyed Lemuria.

Since that crucial lifetime Clare has had some very challenging experiences replaying these same beliefs over and over again in a variety of bodies and situations.

You have been the victim of injustice in many lifetimes and are carrying an energetic vibration that attracts it to you still. This is a theme from many incarnations. You have been 'set up' and blamed for things you haven't been responsible for and treated unfairly. You have been imprisoned and tortured because of the actions of others.

When I met Clare the limiting thoughts that had held her soul captive over many thousands of years were ready to be released.

I worked with Clare twice. In between sessions she had a recurring vision of Lemuria sinking beneath the waves. I asked St Germain to remove her beliefs and their vibrational imprint from the cells of her body and her energy field and guided her in a powerful visualisation where she threw the scroll documenting that lifetime into a fire.

I replaced the old energy with the high vibration Christ Consciousness energy and helped her to see herself as she really is.

You have always carried the light and the wisdom of shamanic energy. You are a highly evolved soul and were part of the forces of light in Lemuria for a reason. You have unique abilities but have not been able to fully express these in your many lifetimes since. These talents and gifts are the essence of who you are. The obstacle you have always faced are the beliefs you have carried about yourself and people in general. These have been a stumbling block.

You started off well in many lifetimes and radiated light and healing and many were drawn to you for help. In one lifetime you let your light shine for the benefit of others at first but then over time the beliefs you have held since Lemuria kicked in and you ended up an outcast, hungry, alone and struggling for survival ... You interpreted this as being treated unjustly but you created this situation yourself with your lack of self-belief and feelings of shame.

As Clare commented afterwards:

These feelings I have had all my life have completely gone now. Since my sessions I don't have them at all. I do still feel *a connection to this magical land of **Mu** ... but in a different sense. I see its beauty and how I was a loving soul of this land at this time. I see myself as a young woman ... who was beautiful and held a 'state of grace.'*

My reading continued:

Your destiny in this lifetime is to carry the shamanic energy again in its purest form and vibration. You will rise up like a phoenix once you have forgiven yourself for your small part in the downfall of Lemuria and learned to trust and accept yourself once more. Your future is very bright and after such a long time of suffering, self-blame and hardship you will reconnect with your powerful, magnificent soul self and rise rapidly like the most beautiful and noble bird in existence. You have great and wonderful work to do. The time of waiting is over and you will regain and use your talents very quickly. It will be a blessed and wonderful time which is all you deserve after years of self-induced purgatory.

Clare commented on this as well:

Wow ... the ending to the vision that Chris was leading me through was incredibly powerful. There was a fire and I threw the Mu scrolls into it, then jumped in too. Then out of this fire ... rose ... a phoenix. The colours were extraordinary and there was so much light that the turquoise green and yellow sparkled like jewels catching the sun. It was incredibly powerful as well as beautiful.

It has been several years since these sessions with Clare. When I contacted her, to ask for permission to tell her story, she sent me this email:

I had no idea the work I did with you would completely clear and release the many lifetimes that had made me feel unworthy, distrustful and incapable. The process didn't happen immediately but all I can say is, I do not recognise the person I was four years ago. It is hard to remember that person, living with the imprint of alternate life bleed-throughs that had shackled and kept me energetically chained up for my entire life. The emotional pain I carried from others suffering from my mistakes and decisions in other lives was unbearable. My life hurt. I didn't know why I felt such pain. It was always with me and it got worse as I got older. People always said I looked as if I had the weight of the world on my shoulders and that is exactly what it felt like.

As I related in Chapter 7, the change in Clare has been so great that her life purpose has also changed. In Clare's words,

Working with the disadvantaged was one of the possibilities available to me. What I discovered was that once I healed from my hurt, I did not want to engage on that energetic at all. My victimhood has been erased. I live joyfully and abundantly now and am studying for a Real Estate ticket. This is a complete turnaround for me and something I would not have contemplated in the past.

Over the last few years I have been grateful to Kryon, channelled by Lee Carroll, for confirming many of my intuitive beliefs. Kryon talks of the intelligence of every single cell of our bodies and labels the part of each cell that remembers and holds the wisdom as 'the innate.' The shivers we sometimes feel as our bodies and, in particular, each cell confirms the truth of a feeling or statement is an example of the innate in action.

Kryon also talks of the healing potential of talking to our cells with intention and love. He says our cells want to be told what to do and that we can re-programme them by giving them new instructions. He says it takes a while for our cells to replicate and this is why it takes time for changes to occur. Recently I have been opening my Akashic Record every day and talking to my cells. I ask them to work with me to heal and to:

» Please remember lifetimes where I was free of sinus infections and asthma and had a healthy and fully functioning immune system.

» Be fully restored to a state of full health, optimum functioning and perfection.

I neglected my body for years. It was like a friend I took for granted and failed to appreciate who one day said "enough is enough" and deserted me. I became unwell and struggled to recover. I began to talk to my body. Like someone who has been mistreated it ignored me at first and then one day when it was happy because I was out on a walk, it answered me back. " I don't trust you," it said. I did not blame it one little bit! For years eating has been my addiction of choice and I have frequently ignored its pleas to eat healthily and to exercise.

I have been working hard to patch things up and to get my relationship with my body back on track. I have openly declared my love and listened to what it has to say and it has started to listen to me. My energy levels have risen and my health has improved. I have been experimenting with these soul/cell healing techniques with several of my clients and the results are encouraging.

The energy of the Akashic Records combined with the crystalline, solar light which has been hitting our planet in increasing waves of intensity in recent years is opening up many new and exciting healing possibilities. As discussed earlier, it is activating aspects of our DNA that served no purpose in the lower vibration energy of the past. Working with and within these multi-dimensional layers, miracles are possible. We can work on a soul level.

In partnership with our cellular intelligence we can let go of the distortion and limitation stored within the cells and water within our bodies and in our energy fields. We can go to the source of our dis-ease and rid ourselves of it forever. We can re-programme our bodies using the power of words, carefully chosen and spoken with intention and can transform our lives.

Unexplained medical miracles are occurring all around us and there will more of them as the full template of our DNA potential is activated and returned to us. Being in our Akashic Records, accelerates this process and enhances any healing taking place.

The Akashic Records can help us to release and heal from the multitude of experiences we have had in our human lifetimes. The magic of the Akashic Records lies in their high vibrational and healing energy which can be used to understand and release the past and to harness our potential for the future. Any healing is possible in the Records with the power of faith and purity of intent. Their energy instantly transports us to a healing place and activates the healing potential of their physical counterpart within our cellular DNA. After thousands of years of being locked in fear the Akashic Records are helping us come home to love.

Chapter 13
The Magic of the Akashic Records

The energy of the Records is not only helpful for healing and releasing but as a tool for personal empowerment. I am using the Akashic Records to reconnect with and reclaim talents and attributes from other lifetimes and am teaching others how to do this as well.

Kryon calls this process, 'Mining the Akash.' When I taught my Heart to Heart Course I urged parents to, "Find the gold and focus on it." Nathaniel Branden, a pioneer in the field of self-esteem, encouraged parents to be like miners prospecting for gold. I loved this idea and implored parents to notice their children's unique gifts and abilities and to reflect these back.

When we 'mine our akash' we open our Akashic Record to find the gold in our timeline. Within our cellular structure and the auric field surrounding our bodies lies not only the imprints and residue from lifetimes of trauma but the gems we have acquired along the way. In this treasure chest there are glistening jewels: talents, gifts, personal qualities and positive memories. Nothing is ever lost. If a lesson has been mastered we don't need to learn it again. We can reconnect with our sacred knowledge and with past lives where we had abilities, attributes and positive experiences that can help us now. We can draw on past soul experiences to help us in the present. Once we are in our Akashic Record it is easy to activate and anchor these old memories and skills. It is time to dig up this buried treasure and to use it to transform our lives. We can do this by speaking to the cells of our body in this way:

"I connect with the innate in the cells of my body and ask that they remember lifetimes when I was [eg: fearless, physically healthy, a leader]"

This process is more powerful if conducted within our open Akashic Record.

At workshops I ask participants to make three lists of:

(1)   Their soul gifts and talents.

(2)   Qualities and attributes it would be helpful for them to have right now.

(3)   What they would like to create or draw into their lives.

When I opened my Akashic Record and asked about my soul gifts and talents, I found I had leadership, writing, teaching, speaking and healing abilities and a talent for mentoring young people. In writing this book I have needed self-discipline, resilience, confidence, patience and self-belief and I have asked for these to be reactivated and anchored within my physical and energy bodies. When I do this exercise I also mention things I would like to be experiencing in the present. I ask that I remember lifetimes where I have:

»   Been fully aligned and healthy in mind, body and spirit.

»   Loved unconditionally.

»   Had healthy relationships with others.

»   Manifested abundance in all areas of my life.

»   Had the confidence and determination to achieve

my dreams.

» Demonstrated will-power and self discipline.

» Been a role model and inspiring leader to others.

» Had a peaceful, safe and fulfilling life.

» Been fearless.

» Successfully completed my soul's mission.

The exercise I teach in workshops involves talking to the cells of the body daily to reactivate the positive memories from the past through the repetition of the words and phrases on the lists. As each word or phrase is spoken our cells and energy field absorb their vibration and over time come to resonate with it. If it is our wish to become determined, tolerant and compassionate for example, repeating these words and activating and anchoring them energetically in our body makes it happen. We literally become these things. Being compassionate (or whatever we want to link in with) becomes part of our cellular structure. Since I have been 'mining my akash' I have had renewed inner strength and momentum and the feeling that something powerful is connecting up inside me.

Working within our Akashic Record there is huge potential to reactivate ourselves to leave behind the negative programming of past lives and to tap into positive memories, skills and abilities. If we do this consciously and intentionally we can easily and magically overcome the obstacles which have blocked our path in many lifetimes and more easily reach our potential in this one. The more we are in our Akashic Record the more we are connected to our soul and the magnificence and power of who we really are. At this time on Earth as we traverse the divide from the Third to the Fifth Dimension and move beyond our human limitations to the expansive landscape of our soul, the Akashic Records can provide us with invaluable assistance.

I am enjoying experimenting and am constantly thinking of new and creative ways to 'mine the akash'. I am using it to improve the ill health I have suffered from for the last eight years. As I have mentioned, about the time Alice was attacked at the age of 16, I developed asthma and then sinus troubles which have persisted ever since. Recently I have begun to go into my Record to reconnect with the past and bring forth cellular memories of lifetimes where I have been free of these physical challenges.

I encourage my soul history trainees to make the Akashic Records an integral part of their lives. The Records are not something esoteric and out there, hidden away in a box marked 'spirit' to be brought out on special occasions, they are there to be used daily in practical ways to help us. They can protect, uplift and calm us. Being in the Akashic Records is the best stress relief I know. I encourage those I teach to spend time every day in their Akashic Record, to be in them at work and in them when dealing with difficult people or situations.

With the help of the Akashic Records we can rise above human drama and pain and see things from a higher and more detached perspective. We can use them to let go of anxiety and of all that is holding us back. We can use them to access our full potential. I suggest to workshop participants that they have a copy of the Access Prayer on their phone, in their handbag and in their desk at work. These tools are life changing and are supposed to be used. The Akashic Records, once accessible to an elite few, are now available to anyone with the pure intention to use them in positive ways to benefit themselves and others.

Recalibration is the process of bringing our mental, physical, emotional and spiritual bodies into alignment. It is changing our human composition or form. It works on the DNA within our cells to lay down a new blueprint. For the old souls on the planet this process in the last few years has been testing. The increasing waves of light have accelerated the process of changing our Third Dimensional carbon based bodies to Fifth Dimensional bodies of crystalline, solar light. This balancing out is affecting us on every level. Any area we have neglected is being highlighted. What we have been avoiding has become impossible to ignore. If we have been hiding from emotional issues these are what we have had to confront.

If we have been taking our bodies for granted this weakness has manifested in physical ailments and discomfort. Recalibration is not much fun as it takes us out of centre and into a void, a 'no man's land' where we question our beliefs and our very existence, but this is necessary to create a new human template within our DNA, a template that will bring even more magic and miracles into our lives. As a friend said to me when I was in the eye of the recalibration storm, we should welcome these energies as they are a sign that we are evolving.

The Akashic Records are an oasis in the desert as I go through this process. They are here to help us make this transition in comfort. The Akashic Records are not something to be studied and then forgotten about. They are a gift to help make our human lives easier, to bridge the gap between Heaven and Earth and to help us move with ease and grace into a higher consciousness and new way of being. Once we have made the transition into this multi-dimensional **quantum energy** it will be even easier to reach across time and space to access the precious gems of our soul heritage and to alchemically transform this glittering gold from energetic potential into reality.

Recent chaotic and unpredictable weather patterns and earthquakes are a sign that the recalibration process is happening for Earth as well. The **planetary grids** are realigning to harmonise with our new template. Patricia Cota Robles as part of *The Living* *in Oneness Summit* in May 2014, talked of the process the Earth is going through as we transcend our fear based consciousness and transmute the distortion, dis-ease and pain of the past. As higher vibration energy pours into the planet with increasing intensity, the **Elemental Kingdom** is working with the power of air, earth, water and fire to clear all negativity.

This process the Earth is going through is being mirrored by each of us and we are being prompted to bring ourselves into alignment. On a human level those of us who are veering off track or who have a special mission are facing wake-up calls that are impossible to ignore.

One Sunday late in November 2013 my son, Hugh, phoned me. He is now twenty-three and lived at home until he was eighteen when he began university and went flatting with friends. We live in the same city and we keep in touch. He is busy with his studies and a part-time job as a kitchen hand. He is independent and has many friends and we see him when we can. He was uncharacteristically anxious as he told me he had a problem with his legs. They wouldn't stop moving, he said. He added that it was impossible to relax and difficult to sleep and that the previous night during a party at his house he had stayed in his room because he wasn't enjoying it.

Alarm bells went off! This was so unlike my chilled out, fun loving son. Over the next few weeks we did all we could to find the source of the problem which his doctor decided was 'restless leg syndrome.' It seemed to fit with his lifestyle of too much coffee and alcohol and too little sleep. The doctor prescribed magnesium and I brought every product imaginable to help ease his discomfort but nothing worked. By Christmas he felt so unwell that he was sleeping at our family home most nights. He was definitely NOT himself and I was very worried. He returned to the doctor who gave him addictive pharmaceutical tablets which I begged him not to take. Being Alice's brother and remembering how the medication she was prescribed at seventeen seemed to exacerbate her symptoms he threw them away.

Marty and I hoped that seeing his cousins at Christmas would bring him back to life but Hugh spent most of his two-day break sleeping. We were joined in our anxiety by my mother and sisters who all agreed there was something seriously wrong. Over Christmas Hugh started complaining about deteriorating eyesight (he had suddenly needed glasses in October), hearing and headaches. We joined the dots and decided his problem could be neurological. I planned to take him to a neurologist once the holiday week was over. On the 28th of December he phoned me from his work. He could barely see to cut up vegetables and his boss was sending him home. His doctor was on holiday so I took him to the Emergency Department of the hospital.

During my workshops at the end of 2013, I heard myself saying several times, "You never know what is around the corner. Life is full of surprises. Things can change in an instant." I like to talk a lot. It's time I listened more carefully to what comes out of my mouth! If I had done this I would have been better prepared for what was to come.

It was a long day at the hospital. Hugh was extremely uncomfortable, unable to settle and paced continuously around the cubicle. It took me back to when he was eighteen months old and seriously ill with rotavirus. Several days of vomiting and diarrhoea so dehydrated his small body that he was rushed to hospital. For two days he lay like a limp rag and then suddenly, miraculously came alive again, shaking the bars of his cot with a vengeance. Here he was 20 years later, in the same hospital, again like a caged animal desperate to be free. When we first arrived we were told it would be "impossible for Hugh to have a CT scan at this time of year." I watched the expression on the House Surgeon's face change as he questioned Hugh and asked him to repeat his symptoms. A CT scan was quickly arranged and we waited for the results.

Later that night we were told that Hugh had a brain tumour of the pineal gland. Alice, Mary, Marty and I were there to hear the news and to see on screen the unmistakable shadow in his brain. I was shocked! Even after my experiences with Alice I am an optimist. I don't like to think the worst or even go there in my mind. I was sure lightning couldn't strike twice. We had been through so much as a family.

My children are my weak spot, my Achilles heel. I adore them. What hurts them hurts me too. I was devastated! In 2004 we had been on a holiday to the Gold Coast of Australia. We discovered a family passion for roller coasters and still have a photograph of the five of us at the top of a ride, poised to go down. I often look at that happy photo and think what a good thing it was that we had no idea what would be coming our way or of the hair raising ride we would soon be on. Here we were again sitting atop another potential roller coaster. I could not believe it!!

My sister took another photo of the five of us. We are still smiling but look subdued and stunned. My joke "Family bonding for the Wilsons ... spending time at Wellington Hospital," made everyone laugh, even Hugh. We left him tucked up in bed. He was still uncomfortable and restless but hopeful that now the problem had been identified the doctors would find a solution.

The next morning I was up early and I forced Mary onto a bus heading to a northern beach town where she planned to spend New Year's Eve. She has spent enough time in hospitals in her young life visiting Alice and being swept up in the ensuing drama and sadness that Marty and I felt she didn't need another week of it. My sisters were holidaying at the same place so she had support if she needed it.

At the hospital, Hugh had an MRI scan and was getting ready for surgery. We were told his situation was critical because he had hydrocephalus, a build-up of fluid in his skull caused by the tumour which was stopping the flow of cerebrospinal fluid. Hugh had hated the MRI scan as with his leg issues he found it impossible to keep still but he was in good spirits. I was delighted to see his sense of humour had returned. I marvelled at his courage and strength of character as he thanked the hospital staff and kept them entertained. He showed no fear or self-pity but kept asking everyone else if they were okay. I was extremely proud of him.

Hugh gave the thumbs up as they wheeled him off to theatre and Marty and I went to the hospital chapel where my twin sister was waiting. Hugh was thoroughly briefed before the operation and warned of the possible dangers. The tumour was buried deep in his skull near a major artery so we knew the operation would not be straightforward. Everything had happened so fast that we didn't have time to focus on the seriousness of Hugh's situation or what could go wrong—which was a good thing. I sat in the chapel and prayed, doing my best to channel healing energy his way. I enlisted the spiritual hierarchy to help and prayed for the skill of the surgeons. They had briefed us on what they hoped to achieve. Draining the fluid was most important as Hugh was in danger of having a seizure. They also hoped to remove some cysts and take a biopsy of the tumour. I felt connected to my son and then I felt his consciousness travel out into the ethers and realised the anaesthetic had kicked in.

Trust has been a core learning for me in this life. My trust and faith were tested over the next four hours. It was an agonising wait until the surgeon phoned us to say the operation was over and that he felt it had been a success. For the rest of the day Hugh was tired, groggy and disorientated but when we arrived to see him the next day, which was also his twenty-second birthday, he was feeling better than he had in weeks. The 'restless legs' were gone, his headache was gone and his vision and hearing were much improved. It was the best birthday present he could have wished for. By the end of the week Hugh had been discharged from hospital, was back home with us and rapidly recovering.

I am proud of the way we coped with this latest roller coaster. When I compare how we reacted to our family crisis seven years previously I can see how far we have come. The wisdom and strength we have gained through Alice's illness have been invaluable. We have learned to 'let go and let God' and that fear in any shape or form does not help. We did not step into fear and I am proud of that. Hugh made this easier. He was open to the healing efforts of myself, my sister Judy and others, and remained unfailingly gracious and positive. He was an inspiration.

Alice has also taught me the value of staying in the present. For the first three years of her illness my first thought of the day was always, "Will this be the day Alice kills herself?" For self-preservation I had to learn to live in the moment and this was useful training as we waited for over three weeks for the results of the biopsy. A huge outpouring of love and support from family and friends also helped me cope but so did the Akashic Records. It was hard having two out of three children with lives under threat. For me, their mother, the Akashic Records were a life raft on a stormy sea.

The question in everyone's minds was, "Is the tumour cancerous?" In late January 2014, we were told that it was. Hugh had a malignant, aggressive tumour of a rare kind. Called a germinoma it occurs in one in a million people and is curable. Ninety percent of sufferers recover completely. There was more good news. Hugh would not be having another operation. His tumour could not be removed surgically as it was too deep and would be treated by radiation. A lumbar puncture and MRI scan revealed there were no cancerous tumours or cells in other parts of his body so chemotherapy would not be necessary. We were ecstatic!

Thanks to the Records I was able to stay calm and positive. Hugh gave me permission to access his Akashic Record to find out what was happening. I was able to see the bigger picture and to trust that all was well and happening for the highest good of us all. The information in his Record was reassuring.

I was relieved and delighted to find:

» That Hugh's life is not supposed to end in his early twenties. That his illness is a wake-up call and an effort by his soul to get him on track and to open him up to his life purpose.

» That it is no accident that the tumour was around his pineal gland, also known as 'the seat of the soul.'

» Who Hugh really is (a starseed and esteemed member of the Galactic Council).

» That his life purpose is to work globally to help humanity change in consciousness.

The most important thing the Akashic Records have taught me is when we are struggling on a human level, on a soul level it is perfect. I have come to see and appreciate the gifts for all of us in Alice's illness and how this situation has delivered many of our chosen lessons and perfectly prepared the five of us for our respective missions. This experience has taught me to trust the process of life and to trust that whatever happens is meeting the needs of our soul and helping us to evolve. There is a higher purpose to everything that happens and many different layers. Nothing is as it seems.

At the significant age of 22 this situation has helped Hugh step into his true identity. He has an important job to do during this lifetime and his soul is getting him ready for this. During his illness there have been many glimpses of the beauty and radiance of his soul and his true self. He has had to step up and has passed with flying colours. The rest of us, Hugh's family and friends, have been tested and given the chance to reveal our authentic selves. We have been challenged to step out of fear and into love. My magnificent and much loved Hugh has led the way. My sister, Judy, tells me that Hu is "the sacred sound of God." I now know why I felt compelled to give that name to my special son.

As I write this we have just received the results of Hugh's post radiation MRI scan. The tumour has completely disappeared! The before and after pictures of his brain are a sight to behold. Our faith and Hugh's courage have been rewarded and thanks to this miracle he can now get on with his life.

Recently I worked with a young man, via Skype. He wants to create something great in this lifetime. He is propelled by an inner force to make his mark. His passion is environmental issues and I could see he has the drive and the determination to make a difference. His Akashic Record revealed why he has such a burning desire to succeed. In his recent lives he has lost his way. Starting his journey full of hope and optimism, he has in lifetime after lifetime failed to reach his destination. He came to me frustrated, angry and almost defeated.

A true **Indigo Child**, he was impatient, angry, questioning and delightful. He challenged me for answers. In his Akashic Record I could see a clear picture. He has the potential to make a valuable contribution to the world and this is the higher purpose of his life but he has important lessons to learn around trust and patience and not trying to force things to happen. He became frustrated with me as I told him that he was on course but it would take longer than he hoped because certain things needed to happen first. I explained that for those of us with a big job to do it often takes longer to be successful because our foundations must be strong. To be earthquake proof 'our house' has to be built on solid ground and we have to be fully prepared for the task. I encouraged him to stop trying so hard and to surrender to and trust in the process.

In the energy of the Fifth Dimension the intentions we hold have to manifest into form. This is not a linear process. It is hard to understand this from a Third Dimensional perspective when A is followed by B then C, D and E. We have the end in sight and do everything by the book to reach our goal. Step One followed by Step Two but still it eludes us. Why? The timing isn't right. The energy is not aligned. We are not up to the task. Our soul wants us to succeed and knows what has to happen first.

If we focus on abundance and then expect our income to increase immediately we may be disappointed. Our soul may see that before we can make money we have to raise our energy, improve how we relate to people and learn some lessons. We find ourselves on a steep learning curve and amidst the turmoil feel angry and disillusioned because the universe is not giving us what we want. What we fail to realise is that the universe is setting the energy in motion so we are able to create what we want.

We may put out a call for more money to pay our bills and expect a surge in client bookings but nothing happens. Dejected we go for a walk and while we are out we get a money making idea that can bring in much more income than regular one-on-one clients. This is how the universe works. It is not linear. It is not predictable. This energy of the New Earth is multi-dimensional quantum energy and we have to trust it. It can go from A to Z to F to Q and back again. It is a benign energy which works with our soul to help us to successfully fulfil our chosen mission in life.

I spent years teaching parenting and started writing a book on the subject. I dreamed of being a well known parenting authority. My ideas were good. My motives were pure. I had the passion and achieved a modicum of success but never the lofty heights of my dreams. Now I am starting to see where the pieces of the puzzle fit.

My parenting work was not about me becoming the latest guru. It meant that when Alice became ill I didn't blame myself (I knew I had been a conscious and conscientious mother) and I learned techniques which I could use with her. When Alice was seriously unwell I had to dig deep and use my most effective tools and strategies. Also the years of running workshops mean that speaking and teaching now come naturally to me.

Our soul knows what our plan is. It sees the bigger picture and is determined to make our dreams a reality. It has the end in sight and wants us to get there. The route we take is often not a direct one, especially now we are letting go of so much that has weighed us down during our lifetimes on Earth. Like the quantum beings we are, we have been all over the place. It has been two steps forward, one step back and we have lost our way at times. Like a tramper lost in a storm we must trust that our soul knows the way and let it guide us. The good news is our days of being lost in the wilderness are over because for the first time in many lifetimes we are living in energies that support and nurture us.

Alice is an amazing soul and I know her higher self is desperate to help her to heal from the trauma of the past and to do the work she came here to do. She has allowed me to check this in the Records and I am humbled and thrilled by the potential for her future. As I said to my Indigo client," Those who face the toughest challenges often reach the greatest heights."

Alice has spent at least five of the last seven years in psychiatric hospitals and therapeutic communities. She is back in Wellington now, living independently with a flatmate and we see her regularly. Several months ago she had a 'relapse' and was in the psychiatric ward for six weeks. As her mother I felt sad about this but trusted that her higher self knew what it was doing. Despite the numerous attempts to end her life Alice has a strong survival instinct. When all seems lost and all hope is gone, she has consistently over the last seven years pulled something out of the hat at the eleventh hour and manifested the help she needs. The night Alice went back into hospital was frightening and the following weeks were scary as she regressed and was difficult to connect with. My inner voice told me that she was releasing another layer of stuck and toxic residue and that she would come through this stronger and with greater clarity and purpose. Information from the Akashic Records confirmed these gut instincts.

Recently it was Mother's Day. I usually down play it but decided this year to honour the day and myself. After all I have been through I felt I deserved it. Mary is away at university and Hugh was working so I spent the day with Alice who has not been in town for the last two Mother's Days. We had a wonderful time. We went out for lunch at a seaside suburb and walked and talked and our love for each other shone through. I could not have received a better gift. On her last birthday Alice turned twenty-five. Some of her friends came to our home for dinner. She has met them through the mental health system and they all have their story to tell. I thoroughly enjoyed their company. Each one of them is inspiring, brave and special.

After the nightmare of the last seven years Alice is stepping from the darkness into the light and we are right there beside her. I am not the same person I was eight years ago. I love the person I am now and have Alice and the Akashic Records to thank for it. I never saw this coming but I am now glad it did. It has helped get me firmly on track to achieving my dreams.

Spending time in the Akashic Records has helped me in so many ways. I have stepped out of fear and the need to be in control. It has taught me to trust. To trust in myself. To trust in the Universe. To know and trust in my soul and its vision for my life. It has reconnected me to my authentic self and my true identity. The Fifth

Dimensional energy has activated this process and the Akashic Records are accelerating it.

Like Hugh, many of us are having new identities thrust upon us. Overnight his identity changed from a young man, flatmate, university student, part time chef, drummer in the band *The Shadow Blasters*, to a cancer sufferer with an uncertain future ahead of him. Everything from his appearance to his lifestyle altered. My youngest daughter, Mary, left home last year and is embracing her new identity as a University student. She is showing courage as she takes this step into the unknown.

My heart goes out to Alice as she makes the transition to adult life. Changing her identity from the sufferer of mental illness to a 25 year old independent adult is fraught with challenges as she takes a few tentative steps and then retreats to the comfort and familiarity of the institutions that have been her second home at a crucial time in her life. I am grateful to these places and the people in them as I know that without them she would not be alive.

Alice is a courageous and determined soul and I have faith in her to successfully make this transition when the time is right. For someone with a diagnosis of depression the energy in her Akashic Record, the energy of her soul, is lighthearted, loving and joyful. She is beginning to dazzle the world with her presence. It is thrilling to see the 'real' Alice emerge from the shadows.

Being in our Akashic Record helps bring our human and soul selves into alignment. The soul part of us is making its presence felt and if we don't listen and are not true to ourselves ... it steps in to get us back on track, catapulting us out of old habits, behaviours and identities.

So who are we? Are we the personality self we have taken on in this lifetime and honed through years of conditioning and practice—the dutiful child, good citizen, the devoted parent or are we someone else? Working in the Akashic Records has helped me to see that we are much more than we think we are.

Over the last few years, like Alice, we have been letting go of the old. It is time now for us to step into and embrace our new selves. Who we are on a soul level bears little relationship to who we think we are ... we are magnificent and expansive ... and amazing ... it is important that we see ourselves as who we really are ... as spiritual beings with no limit to who we can be and what we are able to create.

Through our Akashic Record we are able to let go of limitation and connect with our soul gifts, talents and abilities and positive experiences from other lifetimes. They open us up to all we have been, all we are now and to all we can be in the future. We are here at this crucial time on Earth for a reason. We have a job to do and if we waver from our path, our souls will take action. They are in the driving seat. They know what they are doing, they know what we are here for. It is time for our personality selves to step aside so our soul's light can shine brightly.

We must not be afraid to leave our old identities behind. For a very long time and through many lifetimes we have forgotten who we are. It is time now for us to 're-member' and to step out fearlessly and to embrace the new. For this to happen we have to first be willing and ready to let go of our old selves. The Akashic Records can provide us with wisdom, compassion and practical support as we go through this process.

I have a client who works for a company selling skin care and health products. Her passion is beauty and regeneration. This is her thing! Not only has she worked in the area of regeneration in Lemuria, Atlantis, Egypt and Greece but in her DNA she holds the secrets to prolonging youth and rejuvenation. In this lifetime she is supposed to use this wisdom in her own way to help herself and others. She admits that she knows this deep down but that old fears are stopping her from moving forward. Like many of us she has a soul history of self-sabotage and of not quite reaching the finish line. It is important that we don't think of ourselves just in the context of our current lifetime. As I told my client she has an impressive soul CV and all the qualifications needed to follow the calling of her heart.

So many of us play it safe and shelter under the umbrella of another person or company. In doing this we are denying ourselves and depriving the world of the contribution only we can make. It is time for us to stop following in other's footsteps and to blaze our own trail. In 2004, I attended a coaching conference in Sydney, Australia and was inspired by one of the speakers, Gloria Burgess. She told her life story and said, "When you go to a party, take your whole selves. Don't stay in the parking lot." Gloria is right. We owe the world our true, complete, pure and unadulterated selves. Every single one of us has a unique vibration which is a gift to humanity.

We must trust in our souls, stop hiding who we are and create the space for our new identities to emerge. It is time to take a quantum leap! Once we have the courage to step into the void, anything is possible. If there was ever a time to offer our gifts to the world it is now! For the first time in aeons the vibration that surrounds us is a match for ours. We are living in energy that is here to support and sustain us, not shut us down.

The Akashic Records are a place of enchantment and possibility. They can help us to release the accumulated pain of many lifetimes and to see the bigger picture and the perfection of our soul's plan.

So ... the Akashic Records are a happy place. Thanks to them I am now in a happy place. Their real magic is the power and potential they have to end human suffering. With the help of the Akashic Records we can rediscover our soul heritage, essence and virtues and understand our soul journey. We can use their energy to bring joy, balance and miracles into our lives. We can go from tragic to magic!

Glossary

Akashic Record: An energetic record of every thought, feeling and experience we have ever had as souls during our lifetimes on Earth.

Aotearoa: The name given to New Zealand by its indigenous people, the Maori.

Archangels: The highest ranking angels in Heaven. They watch over Earth and its people and have different responsibilities. For example, Archangel Michael gives us strength and protection, Archangel Raphael is the angel of healing and Archangel Metatron oversees the Akashic Records.

Ascended Masters: Spiritual beings who have lived on Earth, achieved human mastery and have ascended to the higher realms. They overlook Earth and its inhabitants helping in any way they can. Jesus Christ, the Buddha, Mother Mary, St Germain and Lady Nada are Ascended Masters.

Ascension: A process which is currently occurring whereby Planet Earth and all of humanity are moving from a Third Dimensional to a Fifth Dimensional state of consciousness.

Attachments: Non-physical energetic beings which attach themselves to the human energy field. These are Earthbound souls of human beings that sustain themselves through the energy of living people.

Atlantis: An ancient civilisation which Plato alleged existed in the Atlantic Ocean and was destroyed between 11,000 and 9,600

BC by a series of cataclysms which resulted from the misuse and abuse of power.

Channelling: Bringing through information from disembodied entities or energetic sources.

Christ consciousness/energy: The consciousness that connects us to our god-selves or source that was anchored on Earth by Jesus Christ.

Christed self/selves: Our god-selves. The divine part of us that is connected to our creator.

Codes of Light: The genetic codes carried to Earth by the starseeds. These codes connect humans to their galactic origins and their god-selves.

Cords: Etheric or energetic cords, like tubes, that link us to others via our chakras. These cords can be draining if those close to us are drawing on our energy to sustain themselves.

Council of Elders: The group of souls who assist us in between lifetimes to plan for the next.

Crystal Children: Children who have been coming to Earth since the mid 1990s. They have soul origins in the stars but have lived some lifetimes on Earth. They are natural healers and have great wisdom and an easy-going and peace-loving temperament.

Dis-ease: A play on the word disease which relates ill health to physical or emotional imbalance and discomfort.

Dissociation: The process where to protect ourselves following a traumatic event, we let go of the memories from our consciousness.

Duality: Where there are two different but equally valid realities. Earth has been described as a place of 'duality' as it is a place of sharp contrasts such as, darkness and light, good and evil, love and fear and our human potential to live as higher or less evolved versions of ourselves. Third Dimensional Earth has been a place of duality and separation. The Fifth Dimensional Earth we are moving into is a place of unity and oneness.

Elemental Kingdom: Nature spirits that work with the four basic elements of fire, air, earth and water.

Entities: Spirits that have never been embodied that attach themselves to human beings like energetic parasites.

Family of Origin: The family you grew up in. This includes parent/s and siblings and sometimes other members of your extended family that lived with you during your childhood.

Fifth Dimension: The higher vibration energy that Earth is moving into during this time of Ascension or the 'Shift of the Ages.'

Galactic Council: A group with representatives from throughout the Milky Way Galaxy who meet to discuss its affairs and who provide direction and leadership to the planets and Star Nations within the galaxy.

Hall of Records: A place that is easy for human beings to visualise and relate to where they can view their Akashic Record and retrieve soul information.

Harmonic Convergence: A rare alignment of the sun, moon and eight planets which occurred in August, 1987. This was predicted by the Mayans to take place at the beginning of a new age of higher consciousness, 25 years before the planetary shift on 21 December 2012. It marked the beginning of the influx of light and higher vibrational energy which is birthing Earth into the Fifth Dimension.

Higher self: The part of you that is aware of and carries out the goals of your soul. The vehicle for your soul to express itself on Earth.

Implants: Energy that is placed in our bodies by those from other places and dimensions. These are not always planted with a negative intent but can be placed there out of curiosity.

Indigo Child: The oldest generation of the 'new children' who started coming to Earth in great numbers in the 1970s. They are sensitive, psychic and creative and are modern day 'warriors' with attitude. They are here to expose and to break down old systems that are hypocritical and lack integrity.

Inner Child: The part of us that represents our unmet childhood needs and manifests as emotional intensity and childlike behaviour.

Karma: An energetic connection to those we have shared lives with before. This can be positive but is usually referred to in the context of a debt we feel we owe a soul as a result of our actions or inactions towards them in previous lives. Each incoming soul decides who they have karma with and how and whether they would like to address it. Once karma has been balanced there is no pull to share lifetimes together in the future.

Can also be used to describe your destiny. For example, " It is my karma to experience this."

Lemuria: A continent that carried a Fifth Dimensional vibration that allegedly existed in the Southern Hemisphere before Atlantis. Many Pacific Islands including Hawaii, Easter Island and New Zealand are thought to have been part of Lemuria. This continent was peopled by starseeds who first arrived approximately 100,000 years ago and brought their wisdom and healing abilities with them. They worked harmoniously to create a society of love, peace and unity. Over time their collective consciousness changed to one that was ego driven. This human imbalance caused an imbalance in nature and Lemuria was destroyed by volcanic eruptions.

Life Purpose: The main goal or work our soul would like us to accomplish during a lifetime. This is discussed prior to each incarnation but is only a potential. Many souls don't fulfil their life purpose. It is possible to change our life purpose as we go through life.

Lightworker: Those with a spiritual awareness that are working to heal and to raise the consciousness of humanity.

Mastery: When we have learned all of our human lessons and connected to our God-selves on Earth we will have achieved Mastery and can ascend from the Earth plane like the Ascended Masters, Jesus Christ, the Buddha, Mother Mary and others.

Morphogenetic field: The energy matrix that surrounds our bodies which holds the imprint and residue from other soul and life experiences.

Mu: The ancient name given to the Lemurian continent that predated Atlantis and existed in the Pacific Ocean.

Multi-dimensional: Having many facets. Used in this book to describe the energy of the Fifth Dimension which is the non-linear and unpredictable energy scientists are calling quantum.

New Children: Also called Star Children. The name given to the Indigo, Crystal and Rainbow Children who have been incarnating on Earth since the 1970s. They are here to raise the consciousness of the planet and to assist with Ascension.

New Earth: The name given to Planet Earth as it raises its frequency from the Third to the Fifth Dimension.

Past lives: The term used to describe other soul experiences we have had in a human body that according to a chronological time frame occurred in the past. This term fits in with our linear way of thinking and is easy for human beings to understand. In the multi-dimensional energy we are becoming part of there is increasing evidence that we are experiencing our lifetimes simultaneously with the past, present and future coming together as one.

Planetary Grids: The idea that Earth has intersecting ley or grid lines surrounding it which connect and form a matrix similar to the acupressure points on our bodies. These energy vortices are thought to be planetary 'power spots.'

Quantum energy: The multi-dimensional energy that has come to Earth in increasing waves since 1987 and that exists within the approximately 96 percent of our DNA that has been called 'junk' because it does not make an obvious contribution to our human genetics.

Rainbow Children: Highly evolved souls who have been born on Earth since the year 2000. They are new to Earth and are here to serve and to help change and upgrade our consciousness.

Reincarnation: The belief that we live more than one lifetime on Earth. Where our soul chooses to experience human life in different time frames and in different bodies. This belief is fundamental to most Eastern religions but not Christianity.

Repetition Compulsion: A term introduced by Sigmund Freud where we unconsciously draw similar experiences to us in an effort to process and heal trauma and pain from the past.

Sanskrit: A language used in many ancient documents and writings. It is used as a religious and ceremonial language in Hinduism, Buddhism and Jainism. A modern version of it is spoken today in parts of India.

Shift of the Ages: The beginning of the Ascension of the Earth into a Fifth Dimensional state of consciousness which occurred at the end of four cycles of 26,000 years on the 21st of December 2012.The Mayans prophesied that this would be the last day of recorded history on Earth. It was the last day of Earth as a fully Third Dimensional planet.

Soul: The part of you that is connected to God/source. It knows the divine plan for you and for all of humanity.

Soul fragments: Pieces of our soul energy that have split off in various lifetimes as a result of trauma.

Soul retrieval: A process where soul fragments are gathered up and returned to the psyche to enable an individual to become whole and emotionally healed and integrated.

Spirit guide: Spirit companions who know our life purpose and plan and support us during our lives to reach our goals. Most people have one main spirit guide as well as others who watch over them and come in at specific stages to assist them in their development.

St Germain: An Ascended Master, the Chohan (lord) of the Seventh Ray, who works with his violet flame of transmutation to free Earth and its inhabitants from limitation and fear.

Star Children: The 'new children' who have been incarnating on Earth in the last 40 years, the so-called Indigo, Crystal and Rainbow Children.

Star Nations: The name given to the other Christed civilisations (mostly in the Milky Way Galaxy) who have representatives on the Galactic Council and are assisting Earth with her Ascension process. These include: the Pleiades, Sirius B, Arcturus, Lyra, Mintaka Orion, Vega, Andromeda, Antares and Aldebaran.

Starseed: The name given to those whose souls originated in other parts of our galaxy and in neighbouring galaxies who have agreed to be on Earth to assist as we raise our consciousness. The first group of starseeds came to Earth just over 100,000 years ago. In the last 50 years more souls with galactic connections have come to Earth to assist in the Ascension process—the so-called Indigo, Crystal and Rainbow Children. The Rainbow Children are the 'purest' of modern starseeds, having never lived on Earth before.

Sub-personality: An aspect of the human personality that splits off as a result of trauma which is unintegrated and can sabotage our growth and progress.

Third Dimension: Earth until recently has resonated with this frequency which is the lowest vibration in the Milky Way Galaxy. Ego, conflict and fear characterise the Third Dimension as does a split between our human and god-selves. Earth is in the process of leaving the consciousness of this dimension behind and the human pain and suffering that are its hallmarks.

Tohunga: A Maori priest or healer.

Twelve strand DNA: All human beings have this potential, wired into the approximately 96 percent of their DNA that has been called 'junk.' This unique composition is being activated by the Fifth Dimensional energy coming into Earth. This DNA connects us to our god-selves, our Akashic Record and to many soul gifts we have not been able to access in the Third Dimensional energy.

Waitaha: A race of people who lived in the South Island of Aotearoa/New Zealand before the Maori. By the 16th century they had been absorbed by the Maori people through marriage and conquest.

Bibliography

» Bowman Carol, Children's Past Lives, Bantam Books, 1997.

» Braden Gregg, The Spontaneous Healing of Belief: Shattering the paradigm of false limits, Hay House, 2008.

» Brandon Nathaniel, The Six Pillars of Self-Esteem, Bantam, 1994.

» Emoto Masuru, The Hidden Messages in Water, Beyond Words Publishers, 2004.

» Hay Louise, You Can Heal Your Life, Hay House Inc, 1985.

» Howe Linda, How to Read the Akashic Records: Accessing the archive of the soul and its journey, Sounds True, Colorado, 2010.

» Kryon, The Twelve layers of DNA: an esoteric study of the Mastery within, Platinum Publishing House, 2010.

» Lipton Bruce, The Biology of Belief: Unleashing the power of consciousness, matter and miracles, Mountain of Love/ Elite Books, 2005.

» Lipton Bruce, The Honeymoon Effect: The Science of creating heaven on earth, Hay House, 2013.

» MacLaine Shirley, The Camino: A journey of the spirit, Pocket Books, 2000.

» Millman Dan, The Life you were Born to Live: A guide to finding your life purpose, HJ Kramer, 1993.

» Newton Michael, Journey of Souls, Llewellyn Publications, 1994.

» Newton Michael, Destiny of Souls, Llewellyn Publications, 2001.

» Satori Judy, Sunshine Before the Dawn, Satori Incorporated, 2011.

» Schwartz, Robert, Your Soul's Plan: Discovering the real meaning of the life you planned before you were born, Frog Ltd, 2009.

» Schwartz, Robert, Your Soul's Gift: The healing power of the life you planned before you were born, Whispering Winds Press, 2012.

» Sugrue Thomas, The Story of Edgar Cayce, Revised edition, A.R.E Press, Virginia, 1997.

» Todeschi Kevin J, Edgar Cayce on the Akashic Records, A.R.E Press, Virginia, 2010.

» Weiss, Brian, Many Lives, Many Masters, Piatkus Books, 1994.

Connect with Chris

Chris can teach you how to access the Akashic Records in a workshop, via Skype or in her online course. See the Services and Workshop pages of her website www.akashicreadingsnz.com for details.

hearttoheart@paradise.net.nz

www.akashicreadingsnz.com

Facebook : Akashic Readings NZ

Blog: www.themagicoftheakashicrecords.wordpress.com

Email list and newsletters. See details on my website.

Websites of interest

www.themagicoftheakashicrecords.com—The Magic of the Akashic Records.

www.terrimorehu.com—Terri Morehu.

www.judysatori.com—Judy Satori.

www.eraofpeace.org—Patricia Cota-Robles.

www.galacticnomads.com—Judith Prosser.

www.pinchmeliving.com—Bernadette Logue.

www.kryon.com—Kryon and Lee Carroll.

www.leejohnsonwriter.com—Lee Johnson.

www.alchemyforthesoul.com - Donna Falconer.

Chris Wilson

Chris Wilson is a teacher of History, Conscious Parenting and now Soul History. A mother of three young-adult children, she lives in Wellington, New Zealand with her husband, Martin.

Her career has taken her from High Schools to prisons, Alternative Education, soul counselling, running workshops and writing. A common thread in her working life has been the empowerment of others by promoting self-awareness and acceptance and facilitating healing from within.

The Akashic Records have taken Chris's work to a new level. With her gift for accessing the Records she has helped many people to see themselves from a soul perspective.

Chris is passionate about the Akashic Records and the many ways we can use their magic to improve our lives.

CPSIA information can be obtained
at www.ICGtesting.com
Printed in the USA
BVOW08s2054061117
499662BV00031B/1981/P